Published by iDisciple Publishing,
2555 Northwinds Parkway, Alpharetta GA 30009.

# Melissa

## If One Life . . .

MELISSA LYNN CAMP
SHARES HER LIFE-CHANGING LOVE STORY

"Big or small, I'm willing for it all.
This journey is ours—let's go!"

# Melissa

# If One Life . . .

One Love can change your Life
One Life can change the World

JANETTE HENNING & MELISSA CAMP

*"Only be careful and watch yourselves closely so that you do not forget the things your eyes have seen or let them fade from your heart as long as you live. Teach them to your children and to their children after them."*

DEUTERONOMY 4:9 NIV

# Dedication

*F*irst this book is dedicated to my children, Heather, Ryan and Megan and to Jeremy; the four people Melissa loved the most – besides me of course! She loved you with a fervent, unconditional love that exemplified the love of Jesus. Her greatest desire was for you to love Jesus with all your heart, mind and soul and for you to love one another fervently from your heart. You are blessed to be Melissa's family. Walk worthy of the honor. May you never forget the things your eyes have seen or let them fade from your heart as long as you live. May you teach them to your children and to their children after them.

To my grandchildren, Gracie, Maci, Kenzie, Harper, Tanner, Daphne, Kirra and Kili, and to Jeremy and Adie's children, Isabella, Arianne and Egan. This is your heritage, your legacy, your inheritance, a precious gift for you to treasure and pass on to others. Live extraordinary lives dear ones. Love like Jesus, risk loving others with your whole heart, don't hold back. Strive for the excellency of the knowledge of Christ Jesus. The abundant life is yours to seize.

Lastly to my husband, Mark. You have traveled up this broken road with me never letting go of my hand. It has been a steep climb with many obstacles and perils, but we kept climbing up together pressing towards the goal, the prize of the upward call of God in Christ Jesus. Thank you for never giving up and thank you for praying, encouraging me and always believing in Melissa's book. We are truly blessed to be her parents.

I love you all!

# TABLE OF
# CONTENTS

# TABLE OF CONTENTS

# A Word from Jeremy

*F*or almost twenty years, I've had the incredible opportunity of playing music and sharing my testimony all over the world. By God's grace, I've seen countless lives impacted and truly seen the truth of the Scripture in Revelation 12:11, "And they overcame him by the blood of the Lamb and by the word of their testimony, and they did not love their lives to the death."

I am thrilled that Melissa's mom, Janette, has put this book together so you can be a witness of a heart that was truly in love with Jesus. There is something so inspiring about a life that has been fully surrendered to Christ, and as you page through this book and read Melissa's journals, you'll see just that—a young girl whose heart was fully set on serving and loving her heavenly King. Her love for God deeply impacted me, and I loved being her husband, even though it was for such a short time.

I know you will be ministered to as you read the prayers and thoughts she poured her heart into. And I pray you will be inspired to live a life like hers—wholly abandoned to the Lord and His will for your life. He is fully trustworthy, and even in the hardest of trials He can give us peace we cannot find anywhere else. As you read through these pages, you will see Melissa knew this absolutely, and I pray you will, too.

In Christ,
**Jeremy**

# Introduction

> " *If one life comes to know Jesus Christ as their Savior through what I go through, it will all be worth it.* "

♡ *Melissa*

*I* am Melissa's mom, Janette. It is an honor to share Melissa's life and her journals with you.

I am a mother first and foremost. Even as a little girl, I would dream of my children, imagine them, name them, and create them in my mind. As I grew, I yearned for them. I am convinced this came from God as He was preparing me to guardian the precious gifts He would one day give me.

All my imagining paled in comparison to the reality of motherhood. Love for my child, from the moment of conception, was far different from any love I had experienced. The word *love* does not adequately describe the depth of emotion I felt; there should be another word. I knew love. I loved my mother, I loved my friends, I loved my husband. But this was an emotion so different than any of those. Just as my love for my husband was different than the love for my family or friends, so the love for my child was different than my love for my husband. This was a beautiful, consuming devotion. My thoughts never ceased thinking, praying, and planning for this child. It was amazing, four times over.

God had an even more amazing love in mind when He created my third-born child, Melissa. Her life was to challenge me to know the love of God in a way I had never envisioned this side of heaven. I am forever changed by her love for me, her love for her family, and her love for her husband, Jeremy. But most of all I am forever changed because of her love for her Savior Jesus Christ and His great love for her. I was privileged to see the fullness of God in my child and to experience the love of Christ that surpasses knowledge. He has done exceedingly abundantly beyond what I imagined, and I am trusting that He will continue to use my daughter's life to bring Himself glory in every generation.

*"To know the love of Christ which passes knowledge; that you may be filled with all the fullness of God. Now to Him who is able to do exceedingly abundantly above all that we ask or think, according to the power that works in us, to Him be glory in the church by Christ Jesus to all generations, forever and ever. Amen"*

*(EPHESIANS 3:19-21)*

When I first met Jeremy and knew Melissa cared for him, I began to pray he would become a mighty man of faith. I did not know then why the Lord had me praying that for Jeremy Camp. I had no idea that I would need the strong faith of this young man of God to strengthen me and carry me through my darkest valley. I had no way of knowing that this "mighty faith" that I prayed for would unite with my daughters to carry them to the heights of intimacy with God and would sustain them through the valley of the shadow of death and beyond.

Jeremy has said that God answered his "Why?" question. He said it was so he could tell everyone to "walk by faith and not by sight." Those words are precious to me as I think about my prayers for this now-mighty man of faith. I remember with tears the day Jeremy and Melissa came home from their honeymoon and I heard the completed song "Walk by Faith" for the first time.

> I will walk by faith even when I cannot see, because this broken road prepares Your will for me.
>
> ♡ *Melissa*

"Mom," Melissa whispered, "I thought of those words."

Yes, this "broken road" was prepared by God's will for Melissa, Jeremy, me, and my precious family, but also for the people and generations to follow who will come to know the love of Jesus through her life, her journals, Jeremy's songs, and the testimonies of those who have been forever changed.

Melissa had a great desire to share her life—her struggles and successes—so others would learn to walk in God's ways. I can easily picture her in a small group, teaching teenage girls about relationships, self-image, eating disorders, depression, or loneliness. I can see her around a campfire, or in a dorm room, or with a car full of kids—always focusing them on Jesus and the Word of God as the only answer to their problems. I see her singing "My Father's Eyes" with her face pressed nose-to-nose with her little sister, Megan. I hear her laughing with her older sister Heather and see her being swallowed up in the hugs of her big brother Ryan, and always focusing all of us on Jesus.

As you read Melissa's prayers and journals and follow her journey, you can see and hear the mind of God at work in her, preparing her for His eternal plans and purposes. Prayers are eternal. They are mustard seeds, planted by faith and grown in the very heart of our eternal God and Father. God is continually giving Melissa the desires of her heart by answering these prayers according to His will and perfect timing.

*I look at this diary and wonder what its use is. Do you yearn for me to share it with strangers, loved ones, or just You and I? If someone were ever to read this, I would be so thrilled, thrilled to know that God has used me to share of His wonderful promises.*

I believe Melissa wrote her journals for God, her loved ones, and also for you. My prayer is that through them, you will enter into an intimacy with God that you have never experienced before. Prepare to be transformed as the living Lord Jesus Christ is revealed to you through Melissa's conversations with Him. Glean from her, glean from Jesus, and you will never be the same again.

Melissa's journals begin in February 1997. They chronicle Melissa's four-year journey with God through high school, her first year of college, falling in love, cancer, and her engagement to Jeremy. Her journal entries are interspersed throughout the book so you can share in her life by reading her own words.

As I read my daughter's journals, God is using them to comfort me and teach me. I pray they will do the same for you.

*Eternity has no troubles.*
*Eternity of blessings!*
*So even though now you're*
*having the wind against you,*
*know God knows and sees*
*what you're going through.*
*Pray. Walk away, amazed*
*and full of worship.*

♡ *Melissa*

# CHAPTER 1

## YOUR GLORY IS WHAT I SEEK

*"You want to know what I think? I think I know why we go through trials, or at least why I do. I think the Lord is constantly allowing trials to show me where my home is: heaven. So many times, I forget to look at things with an eternal perspective and then a trial will come. That's when I'm reminded that no matter what we go through or endure, succeed at or fail at, this is not our home. So, with that I want to go through these trials standing, knowing soon and very soon we're gonna see the King. Amen."*

*Jesus, this life I live belongs to You. How wonderful. So, because it belongs to You, I ask You to use it. Your glory is what I seek to please. I want to be a woman of prayer, hidden and even discrete. I want meekness and fruit. I only want You for now. I feel the call to enjoy this servant time alone, single and free for ministry. Protect me from deception and help me to know you more. I'm interested and so willing to seek You. My lover of my soul—You make me whole. I'm in love with You. I can't wait to be with You, but I also can't wait to allow You to reign in me again, in your power.*

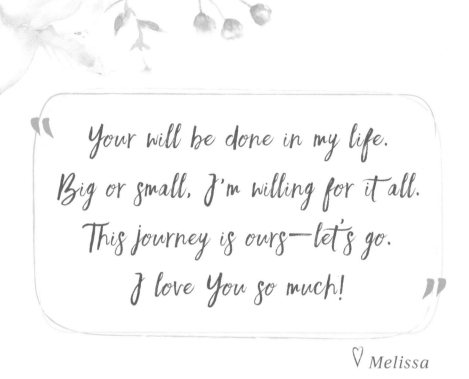

*Your will be done in my life.*
*Big or small, I'm willing for it all.*
*This journey is ours—let's go.*
*I love You so much!*

♡ *Melissa*

*Open my eyes and keep me from sin. I ask You'd speak to me over and over again so I will learn to know You consistently. Here's the beginning of forever! Amen.*

"Hey, Mom, look at this." Trying not to show the terror I was feeling, I gently said to my beautiful nineteen-year-old daughter, "We'll see the doctor in the morning." Her response was, "No, not tomorrow, I have Bible Study." God came first with Melissa.

Fear gripped me. I went into the bathroom and cried as I projected ahead, imagining the worst. I had just seen a huge abdominal mass in my child. As I lay on the floor muffling my cries, my spirit groaned to my God. At that moment, I heard a voice say to me, "Here we go!" I knew this would be the greatest trial of my life, and I knew God was with me. I continued to pray for wisdom, especially in choosing the right doctor.

Mark and I were married January 31, 1976. We were blessed to have four children, and God began to fashion a family after His own heart. Each child He gave us was so unique and needed. It was like a beautiful puzzle to me. Each piece made our family more beautiful, and with each piece God was revealing more and more of the picture He was creating. Melissa was our third born. There was something extra special about this child. Her birth was natural and easy. I was able to leave the hospital twelve hours later—she had never left my sight. I used to tease all the kids that Melissa was really the only child I knew for certain was mine because she was never taken away by those hospital nurses to be mixed up with all the other babies!

I love all my children with an indescribable love. You know, the love that needs a different word because it is so unlike any other love you have ever known. But then, there was Melissa. She was the child that always wanted to be with me. She reached out for me, cared for me, comforted me, counseled me, defended me, served me, nurtured me, ministered to me, *knew* me. She loved me. She was the child of my heart, and she became my best friend.

Now this child of my heart, my best friend, was in danger. Melissa loved God more than any person I have ever encountered. She was a young woman who walked with God. She loved Him, He loved her, and He would not allow any harm to come to her. I knew God would take care of her; I knew He would lead us to the right doctor. I left the bathroom that night facing all my fears. *Cancer.* My worst fear—Melissa dying. I projected ahead to the thought of it, and I could not breathe. No! God would not do that to Melissa—He would not do that to me.

As a family, we had been through many trials—tough trials. We had gone through the fire; our faith was tested many times. We remained faithful to our God and had grown through them. I felt we were like gold, purified, with the dross burned off. God knew that we didn't need another trial of major proportions! He had already given us trials that should have been enough for our lifetime. Now He said, "Here we go." Those trials were just preparation for the one to come. Slowly, I gave all my fears to my Savior. I knew Him. I loved Him. I trusted Him.

The next morning, I called our family practitioner. I believed He was the best person to direct us to the proper doctor or specialist. We went to see him the next day. Melissa's lower abdomen obviously had a mass of some sort. One of his first questions to her was, "Could you be pregnant?" She told him that was impossible because she was a virgin. He did not believe her and told her he had heard that many times before. He gave her a pregnancy test.

Melissa believed in purity before marriage. She lived it and taught it to other young women. At the time she was wearing her purity ring, which symbolized her commitment to sexual purity and was a gift that one day she planned on giving to her husband on their wedding night. When she left the room for her pregnancy test, the doctor told me he thought she was pregnant and that he hears girls say it is impossible all the time, only to find out they are. I told him he was wrong. After her pelvic exam confirmed it was impossible and her test was negative, a very embarrassed doctor apologized and ordered a sonogram to determine what and where that mass was.

The doctor entered the exam room looking ashen. It scared me. Melissa was sitting on the exam table and I was in a chair. I was not close enough to touch her, and I couldn't see her face as he talked to her. The night on the bathroom floor, I had prepared myself for the trial, the biggest trial—*cancer*. But I had not prepared my child. Why? I think I just figured it was a mother's worst fear and that it couldn't possibly happen to Melissa. I didn't want to scare her. I didn't want my child to feel this fear I was experiencing. But here it was.

"It looks like a mass stemming from outside your abdominal wall, probably coming from your belly button. It is too big to actually tell. The radiologist says it could be cancer, but they will need a CT scan to clarify that." I was stunned but okay—I had armed myself for the battle. God had given me the strength to hear the C word and not panic or fall apart. I kept listening to what he was saying, but just wanted to reach out and hold my daughter. The sweetest face in the world turned to me with huge tears quietly streaming down her face. God could not have created a more beautiful person. Her outward beauty was breathtaking; her inward beauty was glorious. She had long, gorgeous, chestnut-brown hair and the most beautiful, big hazel eyes. Even as she was hearing the most terrifying news, her countenance was peaceful and beautiful. Her God was in control.

We walked to the car and prayed. The doctor had already called Mark with the news. Melissa was the one comforting everyone. She held her brother and sisters while they cried. She comforted all of us with her unwavering faith in her mighty God. There was never a sense of panic or dismay. There was never a time she questioned God. She trusted in the same way a little child trusts their parents. She did not doubt His love for her or that He would take care of her. Our church began to pray, our college Bible Study prayed, and as the word began to spread, God's people prayed.

The technicians were gracious and allowed me to view the CT scan as they were doing it. As the pictures came up on the screen, they showed me this huge volleyball-sized mass that occupied my daughter's abdomen. My only thought was, "Get that out of there!" As we left the testing to meet Mark in the waiting room, our pastor Bob Botsford was there. He prayed for Melissa with obvious love and affection. He put his arm around her and said, "God won't let anything bad happen to you." That is how every person felt. It was so clear to everyone that Melissa walked with God. She was a friend of His. She seemed to have a special touch from God. Of course, He would never let anything bad happen to her. He loved her. This was just a trial we were all going through. Melissa would be fine.

We walked over to the doctor's office and waited for the report from the radiologist. It was a very long wait. Then our doctor bounced in the room with a smile. Whoa—what was this? He was happy! He told us that the CT scan contradicted the sonogram. The new report said that it was a cyst filled with fluid, not cancer! Oh, my goodness—what JOY! Of course, Lis would have to have an operation to remove it. Then he asked us if we knew of any surgeons we would like to use. No, we did not know of any surgeons and thought our doctor was the best person to choose a good one. We trusted him. I specifically asked him to please send Melissa to the best, and he assured us he would. We all prayed and asked for wisdom from God to send us to the best doctor, the right doctor when we first discovered the mass. Our primary care doctor was our answer, and now we prayed for him to have wisdom from God to choose the right surgeon for the next step. What joy we had—it was only a cyst! God is so good to us.

Mark, Lis, and I went to meet the surgeon. We were confident that our doctor chose the best because he told us he would. The three of us were so confident that when the surgeon was late and the receptionist offered us another surgeon in the office, we said no, we would wait. We were waiting for the "best" surgeon, after all. He was very nice. He reviewed the sonogram and the CT scan in our presence. It was the first time he had seen them, and he was totally unaware that the sonogram report was different than the CT scan. Contrary reports. We of course thought the CT scan was the accurate one, because that is what we had been told. He explained that he could remove the cyst laparoscopically through a couple of small incisions. Opening up her abdomen would be dangerous, he said, and he went on to explain all the risks.

He assured us that laparoscopic surgery was the safest and best way to remove it. She would have only a tiny scar, which seemed to be his biggest concern. The only way he would open up her abdomen is if it was too big or appeared to be something other than a cyst. He told us his specialty was in laparoscopic surgery. He also said that he would have a gynecologist present at the surgery just in case the cyst was attached to a female reproductive organ—he was not allowed to do surgeries of that type. All the bases were covered. We had the best surgeon, and he knew what he was doing. *Thank You, Lord.* All three of us felt great.

*God, my prayer is to be used by You for Your will. You meant this tumor to be in me so that my friends may come to You. Use me again, use my life. I want to change!*

*The process of obeying God is to do something. Pray in Jesus' name and obey. All of your life God has been doing miracles, Melissa. If you had the proof of the milk and honey, would you go in?*

*Psalm 34—I believe one day I may hear someone say, "Oh, magnify the Lord with me, and let us exalt His name together."*

*Oh precious Lord, Great is Your name. How I know that now more than ever. Jesus, thank You for obeying Your Father and going to the cross, even though You asked if there might be any other way. Lord God, You set the example for me to follow, in different situations, of course. My Lord, when I found out I had a tumor, You had already done a mighty work in preparing me, and I thank You. How wonderful and peaceful it was to know that You had already known and allowed this to happen. But not only that—You waited to tell me until the perfect time, the moment I became willing. O precious Jesus, if I am worthy to be used it's only through You. You make me a vessel worthy of use. I thank You, heavenly Father, for giving me this gift, a rather large cyst.*

"I thank You for allowing this trial in my life because I realize how much You love me through this. I also learned something I thought I already knew. I learned that during this time of weakness in my life, You will be strong for me. And You have been so strong. You have known my weaknesses, failures, hopeless times, and faults, and through all that You have remained strong. How amazing and awesome You are!"

*Lord I just thought of the Scripture where it says that if you were to write of all the things the Lord has done, the world could not contain the books. I just realized in my own life, the things I write to You and say of You on paper are not as beautiful as the quiet moments You and I spend alone. When I am meditating on You and Your Word in my heart and using my lips instead of my hand to cry out to You in every way, those are the times we share our deepest love. So, if that's between just little Melissa, I can't imagine all the unwritten things You spoke of and cried out. Jesus, how special to allow me to picture that! Your lovingkindness is greater than life, and my lips shall praise you and bless You. I will lift up my voice unto Your name.*

While waiting for the surgery, we prayed and were convinced everything would be fine. Melissa and I had some sweet times together. The day before Melissa's surgery she told me she wanted to be strong for Jesus, but she was feeling so weak and afraid. I held her and said, "Oh honey, Jesus doesn't want you to be strong for Him, He wants to be strong for you. He will hold you and carry you through." I reminded Melissa of 2 Corinthians 12:9 (KJV):

> *"And he said unto me, My grace is sufficient for thee: for My strength is made perfect in weakness. Most gladly therefore will I rather glory in my infirmities, that the power of Christ may rest upon me."*

We held each other and prayed. It is a cherished moment for me. Melissa was a fulfillment of this verse. She most gladly had glory in her infirmity and the power of Christ did rest upon her!

Fifteen minutes into her surgery on September 28, 1999, the phone rang in the waiting room. Mark took the call. The anesthesiologist told Mark it was good news: it was just an ovarian cyst. We all rejoiced. Even though we expected good news, it is still so refreshing when it comes, and I thought how good God was to me to have me wait only fifteen minutes for it. Then our family doctor came in to tell us he had checked on her and that it was "just an ovarian cyst."

They removed a couple of liters of fluid.

The surgeon came in after the surgery. He was so excited, boasting Polaroid pictures of the volleyball-sized ovarian cyst. He explained how great everything went, and that he drained and pulled that thing out of her belly button, and that a gynecologist snipped it off of the ovary before he removed it. He seemed so proud of himself, and Melissa was doing fine.

Heather stayed the night in the hospital with Lis. Heather loved her little sister so much. She was like a mercy angel, massaging her feet and scratching her legs for her. She soothed her with lotion and moistened her lips with cool lemon swabs. Heather would do anything for Melissa. They adored each other and would try and outdo one another in showing their love. This was Heather's time to shine and minister to Melissa. What a special gift she was to Lis.

The next morning, they both were so excited to tell me about the nurse that came to them in the night. This nurse knelt next to Melissa's bed, wept, and prayed for her. Later Heather went out into the hall to find her. She wasn't there, and no one knew who she was. They really believed it was an angel coming to them in the middle of the night. I pondered why this "angel" was weeping. Months later, I would remember this weeping angel and know her sorrow. But this night brought a sweet presence from God showing Melissa that He was with her every step of this journey. He showed up strong and was carrying her through.

The next morning, a very dark cloud entered the room. To me, it was like evil seeping in and stealing away our joy. It wasn't the man, even though his bedside manner was lacking in sensitivity. It was his words and his countenance when he spoke. He introduced himself as the gynecologist who removed the cyst. I was confused; I thought the surgeon we saw removed the cyst. While shaking Melissa's hand he said, "You sure went to the wrong doctor. I would have cut you open (he then motioned with his hand a vertical cutting motion straight down her torso) and pulled that thing out whole." Melissa looked terrified. I thought, "Whoa—we did not go to the wrong doctor!" This doctor then told us it was "just an ovarian cyst" and that if it grew back, he would remove her ovary. Then he said she should have a sonogram in about three months to see how things were going. When he left, Melissa was adamant that she would never go and see him! He was a scary person. We all tried to put that doctor out of our minds. Melissa came home and we got to spoil her, which we all loved to do.

A few days later the surgeon called to tell us the results of the pathology report. I had totally forgotten about it. All the doctors were so convinced that it was "just an ovarian cyst" that I didn't give it a second thought. "It's benign, just an ovarian cyst!" Great, of course, we already knew that, didn't we?

*What was that all about, Lord?* I thought it was just a little blip in our lives, a little interruption, another test just to keep refining the gold, another opportunity for us to experience the loving hand of our God, to know Him and the fellowship of His suffering. Yes, that is what that was.

Through it all, Melissa grew more and more in love with her Lord Jesus Christ.

*Dear Heavenly Father,*

*I'm sitting here on the beautiful grass in Del Mar, looking at all the waves rippling to Your desire and tree branches waving in Your wind. I'm watching people walk by with their dogs, sit with their spouses, and fly kites with their kids. I'm seeing all this, and I'm sitting here on the cliff alone. Jesus, I'm hurting because lately I've chosen to go the rough life alone. I don't want to be alone anymore! I want to ask You to be with me. Jesus, I know that I'm even more amazing than this mighty ocean in front of me. I know that because it cannot walk with You, and I can. Lord, may I feel You and know You now like I did when I was sick! May I please call crying out to You today like I so needed to then. How my heart aches and starves for the tender love and intimate affection I felt from You then.*

*Lord, I've told people how awesome that time was, but I don't think I ever told You. When I look back or think back to the time in late September/early October when I had to go through all the doctor's visits and then finally surgery and recovery, I don't remember any of the physical pain. Lord, do You know what I remember most of all? I remember feeling You. I remember being drawn to my knees just to talk to You; to cry to You; to get my strength from You. I remember how real You were, and how I had never known You like that. I remember what peace You gave me. Gosh, Lord, I need that now. I need You now! My tears ache for Your hand to wipe them away. Lord, I know that who I want, and what I want, is You!*

*Christ, I want to put You first in my heart. I want to allow You to direct my steps. But above direction, protection, provision, and so on, I want Your love. I want my heart to be sold out, head over heels in love with You! You know, I feel like my love has been waiting for me—that's You. I feel You've called and written, even sent messengers to tell me You're waiting and that Your love will endure forever for me. Yet, I told You to wait. I sent messages back to let You know my heart wasn't ready to commit. My days weren't ready to be joined with Yours.*

*Well, today I realize this world offers me one thing. It offers me my intense need for You.*

*I want to send You a new message, long overdue, but finally sincere.*

*Jesus Christ, my precious Lord and gracious Savior, thank You. Thank You for pursuing me. Thank You for winning my love by Your true love for me. I know You to be so in love with me, and it's because of that love that I am now so in love with You. Heavenly Father, thank You that You give me the perfect love I've been looking for. Dear God, thank You for loving me so much that You'd continue to forgive and forget all the sins I'd commit that would pull me farther from You. Thank You for throwing them into the sea. I know why the sea is so big!*

*Jesus, what I'm going to say is the
most important vow I will ever say
in all my life. Christ Jesus, my Lord
and Father and Holy Spirit that live
within me, I vow to love and honor
You. I vow to forsake all others as long
as I shall live. I vow to love You in my
sickness and in my health, when rich
and when poor, until death do we meet.*

*I promise to flee from the sins that separate me from You and Your
unfailing love. I promise that choosing to love You and living this
life to love You will be the best thing I ever will do. Christ, I know I
will sin and struggle with understanding how it happened again,
but I pray that my sins would reveal themselves. Show my family
my sins, so I may not continue in them. Holy Spirit, be alive and
well within me, sensitive to a pinprick. I want Thy will and not my
will anymore.*

*Heavenly Father, God above me and in me, please have Your way
in me. I want to see people as brothers and sisters, and I don't even
want to give a second thought to men for me. Lord, my husband is
in Your hands. Have your way and perfect will for Him and me in
Your time. I'm in no hurry to know him. I want to know You! Please
purify Your bride! I love You and ask that You'd radically change*

me. Change my heart to be soft, my will to be Yours, my thoughts to be pure, my love to be committed to You and from You, my actions to be just, and my life to be Yours. Holy Spirit, I know many things that are in me need to be changed, so I ask that as I seek Christ my God, You'd purify, change, and do mighty miracles. Help me to look to Christ and have Him judge me, and help me not to judge anyone. Give me love for my family. I love You and pray for patience to see You work in my life and heart. May I tell no one and just allow them to see I love You, Lord. Help me hear You as I read Your Word. I pray Your perfect pleasing and good will, not my will. All praise, glory, and honor to Your name, Almighty God. Amen.

# CHAPTER
## 2

## LOOKING BACK

*S*o, what was that all about, Lord? What I mistook for a little interruption, a test, a refinement of faith, was a part, an integral part of a far greater work of God that was beyond anything I could have imagined. God had a plan for Melissa, an amazing plan. She knew it, she felt it, she longed for it. As His plan for Melissa began to unfold, I looked back and could see His fingerprints all over her life preparing her and leading her to a time, a place and a person.

*Heavenly Father, How much I desire and have a burning passion for You is something I never want to forget. I don't want to be apart from You in any way, shape, or form. Lord, all I want to want is You—Your passion and love. Help me to search the Scriptures and know You. Lord, be my Lord. I thank You for the forgiveness that You've given me. What You've done for me I'll never know and understand completely until I'm at Your feet. Jesus, I love You and pray for a commitment to You. I want to ask You for direction and love. Guard my heart and put me in the path of falling in love with You. I love You, Amen.*

*I want to love You more than anyone and everyone. I want my future husband to have such a strong love for You that Your relationship with him comes first. I pray and thank You that You have a husband for me somewhere out there. Whether I have met him or not, I thank You for him. I thank You that You have given me a peace about him. No fear. Father, I am of sound mind over him. I pray that my love for You, Father, and my husband's love for You will grow so much that it is the reason for our joy in our lives.*

*I say a special prayer for my future husband. I also say a prayer for the boyfriends I may have before him. Keep my heart pure and my mind as*

*well as his pure. Please have any feelings our flesh would put in our way as an obstacle, to flee us. Thank You that You do not test us, but it is our flesh. I pray against my flesh. Father, give me courage to resist the flesh and seek You, in Your holy name. Jesus, walk with me all the days of my life so I may dwell in the house of the Lord forever. I long to see Your face. Until then, I will seek after You.*
*Love, Your child.*

Spring semester of 1999, Melissa came home from classes at Palomar Community College so excited to tell me about a worship leader she had just met at Bible Study. As she opened the front door, I heard, "Mom, Mom!" and I came running to hear what she was so excited about. "I met this awesome worship leader at Bible Study today. I was worshiping and lifting my hands, and when I opened my eyes, I looked at him. Our eyes met—there was something there, Mom, like an instant connection I've never felt before." Melissa loved to worship. She loved to sing to her Lord, and she especially loved to sing when Jeremy was leading. It was not just that he was a gifted musician who had an amazing voice; there was something else about him.

Melissa and Jeremy became friends within a group of friends who walked with God. It did not take long for Jeremy Camp to be set apart from the others in Melissa's heart. He became more and more precious to her. What was so special, unique about this one? He was good-looking, with captivating blue eyes and huge muscles, but that was not it. He had a fun personality and they laughed all the time, but that was not it. She would tell me it was his heart—first for Jesus, second for Melissa. They were so much alike in their devotion to Jesus Christ. She was awed when he would say, "All I want is for you to fall more in love with Jesus." Wow! He wanted their relationship to bring them closer to the One she loved the most: JESUS! It was what she longed for.

There was an almost irresistible attraction between them. Melissa delighted in telling me about the time they were just holding hands. There was a power, a fire, and a oneness that held them together that she could not fully explain.

They both marveled at the phenomenon.

*Lord, Thanks for Jason and his heart to preach and teach Your Word. I also thank You that he has the desire to worship You. Jesus, when I'm around him and his friends from Calvary Chapel Vista, I feel so comfortable. It's like being home. I feel as if we are truly of one body and family—I love* it. I love Jason's wisdom and gift in teaching, I love Jeremy's gift to lead worship and Danny and Phil's friendship as well, and Charlie's heart for college evangelism. I love it all. But what I love more than anything is that I tangibly see You in their lives. What a blessing to me it was when Jason took me aside and shared that he likes me because he sees I truly love You. Jesus, I do! I love You more than the fish of the sea and even Christian men. Jesus, I love it that You are seen in me. Thank You for that encouragement. I can see Your precious hand in my life, and I also feel the joy of the Lord (You) day by day.

> *I know that the trials and temptations I go through will one day fade away, but You and the maturity that takes place will last forever.*

*Please show me how to spiritually breathe. I want to know You more.*

*Lord, what a day. I guess You're the One I've been wanting to talk to, and I've lacked doing it. Ok, Jesus where to? Do we go to Murrieta Bible College or stay at Palomar? I'll give that one to You so You can make the decision. It's a fun thing to think about going to CCBC. I imagine sitting and learning about You, praying together with other Christian women, and worshiping; so great. But then again, I'm thinking of Nicole and how her heart's desire is for Palomar and reaching out to them. Is Palomar my mission field? Will I be leaving the seed before it grows? I want to be a light on that campus. I want people to come to know You through the opportunities You give me. Jesus, I love the Thursday Bible Study that Nathan leads worship for and Jason teaches. It's an awesome blessing.*

*So how about this deal? I will continue to bring my prayer and supplications to You. I give You my joy of staying and going and my fear of leaving and trust You with the outcome. So, with the knowledge that You have an awesome future for me, I have faith, hope, and joy. I am going to continue to cast this future situation at Your feet, and in the meanwhile, I want to finish this year at Palomar the best I can. I've learned many things this semester, and yet I feel the best lessons are yet to come. Those that have been coming from my downfalls (Jesus, thank You for my imperfections), they make me need You (acknowledge that I need You). I love You and desire to give You my life to be used as You desire. Be my strength to endure in my studies. Maybe Megan and I are to be examples at the campuses we're at. Lord, You know, and that brings me comfort. Thank You for making me the way You've desired me to be, and thanks for giving me the knowledge that no matter what way I go, as long as I am walking with You, You'll use me and Your will would be done (will be). My prayer is that You'll protect me so I may love You all my life. Amen!*

Jason and Jeremy met at Calvary Chapel Bible College and became good friends. Jason was teaching the college Bible Study that Melissa was attending at Palomar College. Melissa loved his teaching and his obvious love for the Lord. Lis had a way about her that made every friend in her life feel like they were her best friend. Boys often misunderstood her genuine friendship and attention to mean more than what it was. Jason was captivated by her. She might be "the one!" Jason had invited Jeremy to come and lead worship at the Bible Study that day. He wanted his best friend to meet Melissa and get to know her because she had won his heart. But from that day, Melissa's heart was connected to Jeremy's.

Melissa had invited all the friends from her Bible Study at school to come to the college Bible Study at our house. Thursday nights our home would fill with college kids and young adults. Jeremy's and Melissa's connection grew stronger and stronger. They couldn't deny what was happening. Jason made his move and got Melissa alone to tell her he liked her. She was flattered, but she didn't feel the same. Jeremy and Melissa were in a predicament. Jason and Jeremy were best friends. She didn't want to harm their friendship, and she didn't want to hurt anyone. She loved this group of friends and felt she was causing a problem.

> *I pray for understanding, Lord. I also pray for Jason and direction. Show him I'm a Christian sister; guard his precious heart from falling in love with me, please. I love him as my brother, and I never want to lose that fellowship. But I understand sometimes we cannot control who we care for. So, Jesus, help me to be discerning and wise in the way I conduct myself toward Christian men. Also help them to conduct themselves in appropriate ways. I desire only awesome friendships with these young Christian men. I pray You would guide me into my husband's path. I pray in Your perfect timing and will, we may recognize one another and the plan You have for us. Jesus, I am so excited to watch You continue to use my life.*

*Lord of my life, I want to write my deep feelings to You. I want to let You hear me tell You about my situations, and I want to get them down on paper. Lately I have been so very blessed. I see how You're revealing Your tremendous amount of love to me. This friendship I have with Jeremy is one I am so blessed to have. Lord, I know how funny this may seem, but it's kinda a weird situation. Here I go (and Lord, I pray that as I'm writing or whenever Your will may be, You would show me what I should do). I feel deeply that Jeremy Camp and I are very much alike. I feel he and I both have a strong sense of faith and trust in You. I see how our hope is in You as well. So I'm not at all worried about us. I feel we both trust You to be our leader in the big, little, and every other decision made. So worrying about that isn't the problem. In fact, I feel Jeremy and I almost are to the point of carefreeness because we trust You so much. Thanks, Lord, that's a rad place to be at!*

*Ok, here's my problem/worry. I know Jeremy and I both want to trust in You and not jump to any decision or clarify any feelings, so to speak. But I'm afraid naturally it will take place. Lord, Jeremy and Jason have such an awesome friendship, and far be it from me to come between that. I know Jeremy's heart's desire is to be the friend Jason needs right now, and I pray that would be the case. My heart's desire is that You, Lord, would tame my high-energy emotions and feelings toward Jeremy. I want to help him to be in a good position. I want to make sure my desire to be around Jeremy and spend time with him and just bless him would only be in a way that gives him comfort so he does not feel in any way as a bad friend, or a friend that's going behind Jason's back.*

*Lord, I pray for Jason and his heart. I ask You to heal any pain he may be going through. I pray You would give him a peace and faith, hope, and trust in You. I pray that his mind would be cleansed of the harm concerning me—that he would feel comforted to know what a dear friend he is to me and many others, and that this minor, yet major misunderstanding wouldn't rob Jason of his joy. Help me to give him the space and time needed to heal his hurts. And Lord, I pray that you would prepare his heart for any hard situation that may come his way. I pray if Jeremy feels our friendship together might grow closer, that You would provide him with the patience and timing to be sensitive not to our own personal gain, but the well-being of our friend, Jason.*

*Lord, I pray now for Jeremy. I feel he is an amazing young man. I see his passion to love You and to live a pure life before You, and I'm blessed and excited for him. I see how young men are drawn to him (and women), and how he grabs the opportunity to glorify You. I see his amazing gift to lead worship and be a leader into the throne room of You, Lord, to bring many to a place of awe and repentance. I see his desire for the Word and knowledge of it. I see his love for others and how he cares for them above himself. I see how he is using the weaknesses in his life to Your glory by learning from them and sharing with others how they can too. I see a fun person who I want to be around. I see an amazing friend who blesses me by his presence alone. I see a very special man who loves You, Lord. How attractive it is to see a man who loves You. I also see how I'm a bit attracted to Jeremy, as well as all the other qualities he has. Lord, help me. I want to run and jump in his arms (help!). I know that would NOT be wise or helpful at all. I can just see it, Lord, he's been praying and then there I am, Miss Stumbling Block and friendship crusher, leaping into Jeremy's arms. That would be BAD! So, since that's what I know my instincts want to do, I need your help. I always need You, Lord.*

*Lord, I would love it if You would search me and know my heart and see if there be any wicked way in me and lead me in the everlasting way. Lord, I want my focus to be on You and how I might be an effective Christian, young woman, and then—let's go! I pray You would make it clear to Jeremy and me the will You have concerning the two of us. But I don't mean we will not be trusting You until and even when we know. I trust when the time is right Your will, will be revealed. So, my Lord, I pray for protection upon our hearts, Jeremy and myself, protection from trusting and leaning on our own understanding. Lord, I love You so much and thank You so much for the awesome privilege and blessings You bestow upon me. You are a giver of good things.*

*Lord, my love is in You, and comparing any man to that is just silly. I will love and trust You all of the days of my life. And my sweet Jesus, will you pray for me and my husband, that we may serve You and not ourselves or each other? Show me and my husband (wherever or whomever he may be) the important things in life and how we can draw near to You and truly live and love You with our lives. Guard us along the journey of singleness until the day we say I do, always putting our trust, faith, hope, joy, and love in You. May I bless You, my sweet Love! Amen.*

*Lord, I've missed writing to You. Something about writing to You helps me pray out more of my personal issues. Tonight, I pray for You to teach Jeremy, Jason, and myself what it is You would desire us to learn so we can grow. My precious Lord, I pray for Jeremy, that while and after Jason and he talk, You'll be filling him with strength and wisdom. Lord and Savior, I pray You would reveal to Jeremy Your will for him. I pray for Jason, Jesus—restore unto him a joy and peace that would surpass understanding. Give him wisdom, ears to hear, and grace for others. For me, I pray I'd learn many things and desire Your will. Help me to bless my friends and me.*

After much drama, Melissa and Jeremy were able to openly be together. Jeremy's love for Melissa was evident, and he was certain they belonged together. Melissa felt the same but was hesitant.

Jeremy asked Melissa to go to Indiana with him and meet his parents. She panicked! Their relationship was moving way too fast for her. She was only nineteen—she was not ready. Her sisters panicked as well, and counseled her to break up with him. So she broke up with him. But afterwards, she doubted and questioned herself. Was she giving up the man God had created her for because she was afraid? There was a connection that she could not deny, and eventually they got back together.

God was beginning to set Melissa apart for a very special purpose. He was drawing her to an intimate level with Him that I am still learning from to this day. She was longing to fall more and more in love with Jesus, and she needed time alone with Him without any distractions. Lis felt that her attraction to Jeremy was a distraction from what God was preparing her for. She told him that, and they broke up again. Jeremy was devastated.

It was summer, and Melissa and Jeremy were set to go on a mission trip to Maui. It was a difficult trip for both of them, but especially for Jeremy. Heather was home from Chico State, and was on the trip to support and comfort Melissa. As an older sister, she was very protective and wasn't in favor of her nineteen-year-old best friend and sister getting so serious with a guy.

Melissa had been transformative in Heather's life, openly sharing her faith and love for Jesus with her. Heather saw the power of Jesus Christ in her little sister and wanted what Melissa had. After two years of college life at Chico State, she left to pursue a relationship with Jesus. She returned strong in faith and ready to serve the Lord on that campus, and Melissa wanted to join her there.

*Dear Heather,*

*I wanted to write you to say what an awesome blessing you have been this summer. You have showed me something very important. You have shown me what it means to have integrity. I see such an honest, loving person in you. So many times, I would get mad because of things you do or say or because you weren't living for God the way I thought you should. But God opened my eyes. He finally changed my heart from conviction to prayer. God helped me realize that you were stuck in the dudu (doo-doo) and all you needed, and need, is prayer and love. I apologize that I realized this so late, but I praise God that He showed me. Heather, I am saying this out of love and truth. I am so proud of you.*

*I know that you have had many tough trials in your life, and I know that God has given you many great friends, but I also know God's allowed that blessing (of friends) to also be a trial. He doesn't give us anything we cannot handle; He always provides a way out of the broad path and onto the narrow path. I encourage you to seek Jesus Christ's face. You are never too far to come back. Never. You are blessed with the knowledge of Jesus; now allow yourself to be blessed by the love and rewarded with joy! He has a plan to prosper you and not to harm you, plans to give you hope and a future, He is faithful to complete all his promises to those who love him (Philippians 3:13). "Forgetting what is behind and straining toward what is ahead." Read 2 Chronicles 7:14 and be blessed. Psalms and Proverbs helped me experience God's will and love. You have such an awesome plan ahead of you. God is going to bless you so much. That's why it's so awesome, because it's all up to us. Receive Him, live for Him. To live is Christ to die is gain.*

*I love you.*

Heather wanted Melissa to move up to Chico with her and go to college there. She really wanted to have that season with her, and she didn't want a boyfriend to mess up that plan. Her advice was to put things on hold with Jeremy.

Meanwhile, Jeremy was distraught throughout the trip to Maui. He called his parents and poured out his broken heart to them, telling them that he wanted to come home.

It was on the trip to Maui that Melissa first felt something in her abdomen. God had been setting her apart for Himself for a while, as is evident from her journals. But even as she deepened her intimacy with Him, Jeremy was never far from her thoughts.

After getting back from Maui, Melissa took a trip to Washington with a family that she often babysat for.

*I'm in Washington looking at all the beautiful things You have made, and it all makes me think of the ones I love. Jesus, You first of all are the first love in my life. I do adore You and want to be with You always. I want to focus on You so that it will be clear to me what it is you would want me to do. I have been focused on myself instead of You. I pray for help so I may delight myself in You. I know and trust You with my future, so I want to lay it all down at your feet. I want to give You the now and focus on this moment and what it may be that You would want me to do. You are an awesome God and worthy of all praise. Help me to be diligent in my work and to serve You with my whole heart. You are a mighty God, and I love you. I pray for my family and for Jeremy, that they would seek you and delight themselves in You. Protect the Neils and I as we are on this trip so we may glorify You. Give us opportunity to tell of Your unfailing love.*

> *My precious Jesus, my life and love I give. Take my body, my mind, and use it to Your glory. Fill me with Your strength. Amen.*

*Lord, I find it funny—seeing so many people walking by; different people than I'm used to looking at—and yet even here in Seattle there is a common thing about us all. We all have feelings, desires, and purpose. Some think that they must be someone that everyone wants them to be. I realize that I am a person that made many of my decisions based upon what I thought others wanted me to be. I realize now that I want to make decisions that will show who it is that You have made me. Jesus, I don't want to worry about pleasing other people to the extent that I don't do the things I want to do. Jesus, I also don't want to have this fear of being who I am. I want to be excited of the person that I am. It's incredible to think that You made me this way for a reason and that it pleases You. Precious Jesus, I want to accept myself the way that I am right now—no even though's or when's. I know I can't live for myself, and I also can't live for others. I want to live for You alone, Lord. I know if I live for You, that at that moment, I will experience all life has to offer. I realize that knowing You is the most precious thing in the world. You are an awesome God, and I love You.*

*Jesus, I hold Bryston and feel this love and desire for a child of my own, and the beauty causes me to be in awe of Your glory. Jesus, I see so many people, married or just couples, and I wonder if Jeremy and I could ever be like that. I wonder if we could ever fall in love with each other and marry. It's something I can't know right now, and for that I am thankful. I want to remember the advice Chuck and Desiree gave me today. Desiree said not to worry about Jeremy and I and not to be afraid of it. That's huge! Lord God, I don't want to be afraid of Jeremy and I being together. I want to take it to You in prayer and trust You will show us the way. Chuck's advice was to simply not worry. Many people when they are older wish they hadn't worried as much, and according to Your Word it is a sin. So, Jesus, I want to give You my fears and worries. I don't want to worry about anything. You tell me to come just as I am, and that I can do. I ask that the Holy Spirit will guide me.*

Melissa continued to have this sense of God calling her to something big, something extraordinary, something amazing. Her focus was on her relationship with the Lord and preparing for the plan He had for her. She didn't want any distractions.

*Lord, adjust me, shape me, mend me, restore me, and prepare me in every good work to do Your will, working what is well pleasing in Your sight, through Jesus be glory*

*(HEBREWS 13:21).*

*Lord, Jeremy came over tonight and helped me see I want You first in my life. Will You take my hand and lead me along the way? Open my eyes and show me Your heart. I want to be pure and committed to You. The things he told me, I tell You and ask for Your wisdom. Much love, Lis.*

*Hebrews 12:1 Melissa what weight and what sin do you need to lay aside? How can you run the race? I want to lay aside men and my thoughts toward myself and replace it with time in the Word and prayer and service. God, I'm so pumped to get to know You more! Jesus, thanks for Hebrews 12:1-2. Knowing You wanted to know if there was any other way than the cross scared me; but now I understand that you died for the joy that was set before You. That's why You endured the cross even though You despised the shame, and now You've sat down at the right hand of the throne of God. Thank You!*

*Lord—I talked to Jeremy today, and it was hard. Please help my desire for You to stay strong. I want and desire You, Lord, and You alone. I want to continue with this desire and commitment. Jesus, I want not to use You as an excuse to end my relationship with Jeremy, but I realize that because of my love for You and because my desire is to fall in love with You, I don't want to be working on any other relationship than that one.*

*My reason remains, one thing is true, I am not ready for a relationship beyond that of friendship. May my husband love me as a friend first and watch me fall in love with You, and in Your timing—when I'm ready—then show me.*

*I want my heart and eyes to be fixed on You, and You alone. Jesus, here is to a commitment to You: My life is in Your hands. I do not know what You're going to do with me. I do know that my thoughts of the future could be wrong. I know I may think we're going to be alone for a long time, and maybe I'm wrong. But my time is Yours. I am the one who is to submit to You, and what a privilege. I can't wait for each moment I have with You. I pray as I'm fasting and praying, You'd reveal to me all my sin so I may surrender it and repent. I want to go the opposite way of sin. Mold me in Your image.*

*I do pray for Jeremy. Lord, I hurt him, and I'm so sorry. I pray You would comfort him and show him the light at the end of the tunnel. Lord, if it would be better for him to go home to Indiana at this time, I ask You would provide a way for him to go. Be with his emotions and heart for You. Help it increase. Help me change and be a woman with Your heart, not a fickle heart. Not my will but Your will.*

*Awesome God—May I take what I've read and learn it and apply it in my life as You wish. May Your will unfold in my life. May I not be too righteous, but humble and meek for You. I love You!*

Thursday night Bible Study continued at the Henning's. Our house would fill with college kids, and this Thursday—the day Melissa and I went to the doctor—was no different. We came home with his words repeating over and over again in my head: "It could be cancer." We talked and prayed with Mark, got ready for Bible Study like every other Thursday night, and waited for Ryan and Megan to come home.

Ryan was in Bible College, and he would bring home a carload of kids almost every Thursday night. Melissa adored her older brother. They were only a year apart in school and always had a very special relationship. Her little sister Megan was a junior in high school and a varsity volleyball player; she was not home from practice yet. Melissa delighted in her little sister. She was her prodigy, her disciple, and her best friend. Melissa poured her life into Megan. Megan and Ryan arrived home at the exact same time. Melissa had wanted to tell them about the doctor's appointment herself, so I asked them to go up to her room. After a few minutes, I looked in the room to see the three of them hugging and crying together. All along, Melissa was comforting them.

As people began to arrive for the study, Ryan had to get out of the house and walk. He went outside and met Jeremy, who was his good friend. They hugged and cried together. Meanwhile, the kids in the house gathered around Melissa, laid hands on her, and prayed. I was standing outside greeting people as they came and telling them the news so they would know what was going on. Everything seemed like a fog—I had no emotions, I was just dispensing information and telling people to enter quietly. Then Brian Pogue, Melissa's friend since they were six years old, walked up. Brian was a special friend to Melissa, and she was very influential in his life. He arrived smiling as usual, and at the sight of him, I burst into tears. We all loved Brian, and God used him at that moment to clear the fog, touch my heart, and grieve with me.

Heather was in school at Chico State, so we called to tell her the news. She desperately wanted to get home to be with us. Miraculously, she ran into a friend and neighbor of ours who had a private plane. She told him about Melissa, and he said, "I'll take you home now!" She arrived in the middle of the Bible Study. As she walked in, Melissa, Megan, and Ryan met her in the living room, where they all hugged and softly cried. What a wonderful sight for this mother to see, my four beautiful, incredible children who loved God and loved each other, holding one another, comforting one another through their tears and touch. No words were necessary.

The rest of the night is a complete blur to me except this one thing: Jeremy and Ryan came back into the house looking exhausted and sweaty. These two brothers, bound by their love for God, their love for Melissa, their fears, their grief, their pent-up frustrations, had been lifting cars! They are both strong weightlifter kind of guys, and they had to do something to ease the fear and panic they were both feeling inside.

Jeremy went home to Indiana as soon as he could get a flight. The day of Melissa's surgery, he called to see how she was and said he hoped I understood why he could not be there. I was beginning to learn a lot about this young man who loved my daughter. He told me that when he was in Maui after their breakup, he had to call home from a pay phone. He talked and cried with his Mom for three hours. He loved deeply, and his soft heart was broken. His family was a source of great comfort for him, but I noticed when he returned to San Diego that he had changed.

Melissa was growing closer and closer to God. She wrote in her journal, "Consume me, devour me." She longed for a oneness and closeness with God in a way that challenged my own walk with the Lord. She was willing to go through anything, to do anything, to give up anything just to draw closer and closer in intimacy with Him. She would say as the psalmist:

*"It is good for me that I have been afflicted, that I may learn Your statutes"*

*(PSALM 119:71).*

36

He was giving her the desires of her heart. The journey they were on was one of intimacy and consuming passion. However, as is clear from her journals, her thoughts of Jeremy never ceased.

*Acts 4:29—Christ consumes my life! Christ makes me go! No matter what my emotions say to me, Christ consumes me!*

*Psalm 69:9—Zeal for Thy house consumed me. God is a consuming fire. Will you allow Him to consume you? Yes! Go big in His power! I sing a song of praise to You, for all that You do and all that You are! Father, You have been so faithful for all my life, from the time my life began until now.*

> *Is God's will for your life devouring you?*
> DEVOUR ME, LORD!
> *Consuming fire! Lord Jesus, have Your way in me.*

*I fast and pray for the Lord to devour me with His will for my life. Melissa, feast on the Word of God and what He has prepared for you!*

*I pray for Jeremy, help him to know Your love and peace and grace and mercy abounding. Help him to not condemn himself, and help me to be what he needs as much as Your will allows. Thank You for bringing me to such a desire for You that I was willing to let him go. Thank You that it wasn't because of sin or a changed heart with him, either. Thank You that it was for a deeper commitment and relationship with You. I fear he doesn't understand and is taking my pain upon him—help his lack of faith and understanding. He is so awesome; don't let Satan get him down. I pray he knows You more because of this. I pray his family may minister to him and mend his net.*

*Jeremy—Lord Your ministry through him and his wife-to-be.*

Melissa missed Jeremy and treasured the relationship they had. Her desire was to remain friends and to take things slowly. We all loved Jeremy. He fit into our family like the missing piece of a puzzle. We were comfortable around him, and he was comfortable with us. Now things were strangely different—awkward, even. His soft heart seemed hard and guarded. Melissa and Jeremy decided to try to talk this out one more time. They left the house to talk, and when they came back, it was even worse. Jeremy stayed for a few minutes then left. Melissa was grieved in her spirit and went upstairs to cry in her room.

Jeremy is an all-or-nothing kind of man. He had told her that unless she could tell him that she loved him, they could not be together. He could not take things slow; he could not just be her friend. However, Melissa could not tell him what he wanted to hear. She was afraid. It was not the right time. She then realized that she had hurt him so much that he had hardened his heart. He could not trust her, and he feared losing her a third time would be more than he could bear. He was guarding and protecting his heart, but in the process was hurting hers.

What hurt Melissa the most is that Jeremy would always tell her that he loved her unconditionally. Over the next few months, she would share with me her confusion over that statement. How could he have loved her unconditionally and abandoned her so easily? She had broken up with him twice; she appeared to be a fickle girl, so it was understandable. However, Melissa's heart had never changed toward Jeremy. She adored him. What had changed was her intense need and desire for a deeper commitment and relationship with Jesus, without distraction. Jesus was drawing her nearer, wooing her into an intimacy with Him that would rock her world. What Jeremy didn't know is that he was always a part of that relationship. Her prayers remained faithful to him while God was fashioning her into the woman of God he needed her to be.

*Amazing to me are You, O my Lord, how every little thing can be directed back to You. Putting a little bow in my hair made me realize the glory and beauty You are. I felt joy to see something as little as that. O my Lord, I know You, and it's what I know and long to know more.*

*The joy of my life is amazing! I will not worry about the little problems that come my way because I know my feet are on the rock and I am in Your hand.*

*Knowing the promises You give, and knowing by experience Your love and faithfulness, makes me go on. You make me want life. You have opened my eyes to the reason for my life. The reason I live is to love You. O Father, I pray with much love today, and beg You to continue to do works in my life that I might know You more.*

*I understand that even though You have done a mighty work in my life, You're not through. I see that, I hear the sounds of angels and see the power of the Holy Spirit directing my life, and I'm amazed.*

*Lord Jesus, I beg You that You would watch over me so that I may praise You all the days of my life—no matter what the days may hold. I give YOU my fear that one day I may love You less, and ask You to be strong for me and faithful when I look to be heading that way. Jesus, thank You for being the sacrifice for me and all my million sins. I couldn't count and love to forget all the wrongs I've committed, but knowing what I've been forgiven for and how much I never deserved that will make me rejoice always. I want to weep at the sounds I hear and the precious time each day gives. Father, I rejoice in how I can know You in all I do, how I can hear and see You in all You've made.*

*Jesus, the emotional bond that we share fills me over, so I pour out of my cup, but I pray my feelings won't direct my walk with You. Jesus, show me the power of Your Word and Your voice through it. Help me see all You want of me. I ask for open ears and an open heart. Continue to make me into the child You desire to see. Thank You that today is a day that I am blessed with. Thank You for my precious life today. The blessings I have are overlooked and unmentioned because of the heavy weight of all my sins, but today I pray You'd make me fresh as You wipe it all away. Help me to see the power You hold out for me to grab, and Jesus, today may I give You all I have. Take this glorious life and child that Melissa dwells in and bring to fruition all Your will. Amen.*

*I want Your will for my life to be done, and I ask that all preparations for them would be done. Jesus, I need forgiveness again, and thanks that I may ask and receive it boldly. The way I acted to my Dad was more than just wrong. I would never want to treat You in that way. Help me to honor my father and my mother. I also pray for self-control and faith. I want to want what You want. So, change me to pray for Your heart's desire, that I may simply know and be more and more in love with You! Amen.*

# CHAPTER 3

## IF YOU WANT ME TO

*H*eavenly Father,
May I hear You. In faith I will quench all the fiery darts of the wicked one. Jesus, I understand that the life I'm choosing will not be easy, but it will be the best life I could have. I realize I am asking You to have Your way in me. Jesus, You know what I will be able to handle through Your strength, so I'm ready, Jesus. I'm giving You my foolish fear because I understand You are with me. I know that my entire life is in Your hands. Lord, in that alone I take comfort.

> *Heavenly Father, You know also if my life or death will bring You glory. I know that my life brings You glory now, and every day I'm blessed to live I will continue to give You glory. Lord, I know You know whether more souls will come to You through my life or death. So fear is ridiculous. Jesus, help me to fear nothing but [respectfully] You.*

*Lord, I don't know why my heart was pounding out of my chest during worship. I don't know either why I'm afraid to go to sleep, but I do know I need You to help.*

*Father, I love You and trust You and know in Your hands I go. Jesus, I'd love to live a long life shining for You each day. I'd love to be made well if I'm sick and shine for You! I'd love to have fun each day and watch You provide! I'd love to see You work miracles and use me. I'd love to impact Palomar's students and teachers to know and love You! I'd love to become all You've created me to be. I'd love to continue to grow more in love with You, Lord. I love Your will for my life. My heart's desires I give to You and ask that You would be glorified in me.*

*Jesus, reign in me, and I pray I'd
run where You want me.*

*I pray that my desire and joy to help in the high school group would be blessed in Your timing and will. I pray I'd be open to the needs I can fill. I pray as school continues, You'd work it out that I either get the classes I need over summer school to apply to Chico in the fall of 2001 or I don't get them and know to go to Butte. You will provide a way. Or open my eyes to Your plan if it's different. I pray for the friends I'll have up there, that we may glorify You and reach out to the lost kids and people to bring souls to Christ.*

*I also pray specifically for my husband, Jesus, whoever he may be—You know, and You also know when we will glorify You best being together. I long for a man to teach me in a new way how to love You even more. I feel it's then I'll know You have given me a life partner. So, Jesus, I pray my husband right now would be learning and loving You more and more. I pray You'd use his life, single as long as it brings glory to You, and in Your perfect time open his eyes to see me. We are in no hurry, none at all. In fact, I'd love quite a lot more time alone with You. So I ask we would be friends for a long time, if I know him now. I want You to have me and hold me, and I want to get to know You more now. Thank You that You hear me, and that Your perfect will, will be done. Holy Spirit, I ask You'd guide me and open my ears and eyes that I might run when I hear You guiding me. In Jesus' name, Amen.*

Over the next few months, Melissa sensed that something was not right inside of her. We remembered that the "scary" doctor had told her that the cyst could grow back and to come back to him after three months to get it checked. Melissa did not want to go to the scary man, so we called our primary doctor and asked him who we should see. He said he would arrange a sonogram and we could decide from there.

The sonogram appointment was very strange. I was sitting in the hall, and I could see the door to the room Melissa was in. I thought she would be in and out quickly, but it seemed like she was in there forever. A technician came out of the room and rushed down the hall. She then rushed back with another person, a radiologist. After about ten minutes, he came out of the room and asked for me. He came and sat with me and just said, "Your doctor will call you." I asked if the ovarian cyst was back. Again he said, "Your doctor will call you." It felt very strange. He wouldn't tell me anything.

Our doctor did call, and would only tell us that the cyst had grown back. "Go see a GYN." End of call. He did not refer us to a gynecologist. We had a terrible time finding a doctor who would see Melissa. Finally, we found a gynecologist that was a Doctor of Osteopathic Medicine that had an appointment available. We picked up the sonogram film and brought it with us, along with all the medical records from her first surgery. But there was another strange problem—there was no radiologist report included with the sonogram. There is always a report. The doctor said she needed another sonogram even though Melissa had just had it done. I asked her if she could just look at it and see what was going on. This doctor did not look at the sonogram and just made the pronouncement that the ovarian cyst had grown back. She prescribed birth control pills to slow its growth.

Within a week of taking the birth control pills, Melissa was in intense excruciating pain.

# Prayers

**Myself-**

1. Seek first You, Lord!
2. Prayer warrior life! Fulfill my calling in prayer, with a joy doing so.
3. Spiritual insight for learning Your Word.
4. Spiritual fruit to increase.
5. Servant's heart to increase.
6. Strength to deny my flesh and pick up my cross and follow You.
7. Guidance and protection from the evil one in the name of Jesus, my Savior.
8. To be led by the Holy Spirit.
9. That my joy may be full.
10. TO IMPACT THIS EARTH FOR THE KINGDOM OF GOD FOR ALL ETERNITY, CLAIMING VICTORY IN THE NAME OF JESUS CHRIST, MY GOD, EVERY DAY. KNOWING IN FAITH THAT I WILL BE A VESSEL FOR MY GOD'S GLORY. FIGHTING THE BATTLES BY GOD'S STRENGTH EVERY DAY UNTIL THE DAY MY FAITH IS COMPLETE AND I SEE MY SAVIOR FACE-TO-FACE. (ALL IN THE LORD'S WILLING PLAN)
11. Health—Lord willing, to be good—protection from any cysts to grow back.
12. Lord willing— Provision to heal my gums as well as strength to endure else wise.

Lord, May I cast my fears to You. Help me, precious Lord, all I want to do is turn to You. May I tell You I'm afraid I'm sick inside? I fear that my body is trying to tell me that something's not right. Help me to leave that fear and cling to Your Word and Your love. I need not worry, for You have it under control.

*Jesus, listen to my silent tears, for through them*
*speak my deepest fears. I love to know that*
*without my words You hear my hearts' cry.*
*Have Your way in me, I want to be willing.*

*Lord, so many awesome Words to live by. I love Your Word. The fact that You love me is enough to give my all to You, but Your grace and mercy chooses to allow me to live every day of my life for You. For You know I'm longing for my heart to be wholly devoted to You. I pray You'd be my love, and if You bring a man into my life or me into his, I pray You'd prepare me to be one with You and closer to You through him. Use me and protect me. I love You.*

We were able to get new health insurance, which availed new doctors to us. After one phone call we had a quick, welcome appointment. The other doctors had failed Melissa and had just given her the runaround.

The new gynecologist examined Melissa and gave her a sonogram in his exam room while I was present. I was so thankful, and didn't understand why the other doctors didn't do this. But this gynecologist seemed unusually rattled. He immediately said Lis needed to go and see a GYN down at their main hospital. He rushed out to call them and set up an appointment. He also sent off her records and sonogram. He then mentioned they had an oncologist. Panic—what? ONCOLOGIST! It was just the cyst back, right? Fear began to grip me, but not Melissa.

*That I may be in Your arms of love, and that*
*there'd be no other place for me.*
*Poem for You, Lord, from my heart.*
*Christ Jesus, Lord, Savior, King*
*You truly are my everything*
*In times of trouble*
*It's Your name I call*
*You won't let me fall*
*Christ Jesus, Lord, Savior, King*
*I truly need You for everything*
*You know this trial that's come my way*
*So, Lord Jesus, be my strength today*
*Help me to give my life to You*
*And have faith to know You'll see me through*
*Christ Jesus, my Lord, My Savior, My King*
*You are My absolutely everything*
*In You I'm content, and by Your will I am blessed*
*Help me now to trust You with all the rest*
*Christ Jesus, Lord, Savior, King*
*Today be glorified in me*

We were so happy to get in to see a doctor right away at the hospital. The doctor had already reviewed Melissa's previous surgery reports and declared to us, "It is just an ovarian cyst that has grown back." I questioned her repeatedly, and she said that it is highly unusual for a young twenty-year-old woman to have ovarian cancer, and that she was positive it was only a cyst. It is very common for cysts to grow back.

There was no rush. She would check with the surgeons to schedule a surgery date. I did not know at the time that this doctor was a resident without much experience. We trusted her to schedule the surgery and choose the right surgeon for Melissa. The surgery kept getting postponed because of the surgeon's schedule and because the resident had decided that it wasn't an emergency.

Melissa began to keep all her important papers from her doctor's appointments in a white three-ring binder. A friend had given her a CD by Ginny Owens with the song "If You Want Me To" on it. It moved her greatly, as it was the exact expression of her heart. She wrote out the words and put them on the front cover of her medical notebook that she took to every appointment.

*The pathway is broken and the signs are unclear*
*And I don't know the reason why You brought me here*
*But just because You love me the way that You do*
*I'm gonna walk through the valley if You want me to*

*'Cause I'm not who I was when I took my first step*
*And I'm clinging to the promise You're not through with me yet*
*So if all of these trials bring me closer to You*
*Then I will go through the fire if You want me to*

*It may not be the way I would have chosen*
*When You lead me through a world that's not my home*
*But You never said it would be easy*
*You only said I'd never go alone*

*So when the whole world turns against me and I'm all by myself*
*And I can't hear You answer my cries for help*
*I'll remember the suffering Your love put You through*
*And I will go through the darkness if You want me to*

*When I cross over Jordan, I'm gonna sing, gonna shout*
*I'm gonna look into Your eyes and see, You never let me down*
*So take me on the pathway that will lead me home to You*
*And I will walk through the valley if You want me to*
*Yes, I will walk through the valley if You want me to*

This song, the prayer of Melissa's heart, was to have a significant impact on her life and Jeremy's. Her heart continued to be focused on praying for Jeremy.

*Sweet Jeremy Camp —Lord, bless him, please. He is such a loving servant who shines with Your love. I ask You to shower his life with knowing and loving You more and more. I pray blessing upon his music record and his band. I pray it would be Yours, and You'd glorify Yourself through it. I pray You'd be protecting his wife (whomever she may be), a cute cookie I know! I ask You'd be preparing her to come alongside Jeremy and help him in his ministry. Thank You for him, and use his life. I love that guy so much and ask nothing but love, peace, and joy to fill his life. Have Your perfect way in him, and protect his life from harm. In Your precious name, Jesus Christ, I pray. Amen.*

*What an amazing love You have for me; To be my King and yet die for me. What amazing love and humility. Thank You, in the deepest way I know how, thank You.*

*Lord, I was just looking through my journal and realized how and why I don't want to trust my emotions concerning someone I may like. Today I sit here as my heart beats for Jeremy, and yet a few days ago I was making it beat for another. Jesus, I see how I need to commit all my ways to You and all my feelings. Lord, I don't want to write down feelings I have of Jeremy if they're going to be as fickle as the wind. So I will pray for him. How I desire blessings for him in many ways. Lord, take his heart and continue to mature it in You. You are such a good and loving God.*

*Lord I pray Philippians 1:9-10 for Jeremy. I pray Jeremy's love may abound still more and more in knowledge and all discernment, that he may approve the things that are excellent, that he may be sincere and without offense till the day of Christ, to the glory and praise of You, our God!*

*I ask for wisdom in whom and when to love through Your eyes.*

*Lord, as I am studying Your Word and desiring You more, I have this overwhelming love for Jeremy. I wish I could whisper it to You, because I feel I haven't been fasting and praying long enough to have an answer. I just thought how happy it would make me to marry Jeremy and go to Bible college. Lord, I definitely need to give You this desire and ask You to bring it into Your will and reveal to me if it is Your will. I'm so happy, and Jesus, I want Jeremy to be this happy. Give him peace in his soul. And show us what to do, as I wait on You.*

*Jesus, I want to give You what's rightfully Yours—my life. Lord, with the amazing love You have for me, I want to show You the amazing love I have for You. I am in love with You, Jesus, and no other. Lord, You are the joy of my life and apple of my eye. May Your Spirit teach me wondrous things I don't know so I may know and love You more.*

*I know that the Lord loves me, so I will live to show Christ my gratitude!*

*Thank You, Lord, for my family, my life, my passions and desires.*

*Jesus, pray for me; my heart is weak. Watch over my family and comfort them and help us trust you 100%. Be now glorified. I love you, Amen, Melissa (like you don't know).*

*Lord, one more day and this pain will be gone, one more day.*

*Monday morning 8:30 a.m. is when I'm going to the doctor.*

*Jesus, if You will, I know You will heal
me, and if You will to bring glory
another way, I trust that as well.*

*I have faith in You to do all and whatever You will to do, for You love me more than anyone else. I trust You and love You. Help me endure this pain with grace, and the pain to come. I know if I have not love, I am nothing. Let's let Your love shine. Help me die to myself so You may live through me. Help me sleep now so my pain will go away and be forgotten in my sleep. I'd love to see visions and dream dreams, so I pray to know You more as I rest. I love You more today than yesterday. Help me love You more tomorrow, too!*

Finally, the surgeon met with Melissa. He examined her and looked at the sonogram. He agreed the cyst had returned and discussed surgery dates. He seemed concerned and said Melissa needed another sonogram, and he would schedule it immediately.

*Lord, I'm so exhausted, but I wanted to thank You. Thank You for bringing me life in You. I know You love me and always will, and that alone brings me joy. You're so incredible, and I'm so stoked to be Your girl! How about I give up and go through this time with You? Sound good? I thought so. I love You, too! You're so precious, and I'll trust You through anything. I just ask for help, and I definitely don't doubt You'll give it. Help me also to see what Your will is. I know I've been planning to go to Hawaii and then move to Chico, but I want Your will for my life first and foremost; because every other way stinks. I never want to hold back from worshiping You. I want to freely worship You, now and always, and I want You to be glorified through me always.*

*Oh, Melissa, how much I love you, you can't even imagine, but need to believe. Allow Me to touch your life so that you may be closer to Me and closer to home. I'm always here with you, never leaving. You don't need to fear surgery or pain. Remember all I went through. I didn't even have medicine. (Ha Ha.) I'll watch out for you, He who watches over you will not slumber (Psalm 121). Let's rock the world and spend time together. Wait upon Me and I'll take care of you. Trust; love Me with all your heart. Deny your flesh, your pride, and all that you know holds you down. Allow Me to be your portion. Allow Me to help you become disciplined and a fisher of men.*

*We have a plan to fulfill together, and, dear, it's a good one. Your husband and ministry will be given to you and him in due time. So, you focus on Me and allow Me to do all the rest. Don't think about whom or when, just have fun with me for now.*

*Trust Me, your future is good. Allow these trials to produce perseverance, patience, and make you perfect. Remember you are My dear child. Before you know it, you'll be here with me, sitting in my arms, and your faith will be completed. So, enjoy life on Earth.*

*Focus on that which I would, that which I led. Don't worry; I'll help you and I love you. If you fail or succeed, I love you the same, so take joy in knowing all things will work to good for you. Seek Me and find Me. Don't fear coming out of your shell. You are ready now; you're not a slave anymore; you're ready to fly. Let's go, dear, and remember a righteous man falls seven times and gets back up. So, trust me, expect to fall but get right up. Let's go, my dear child, and do it all with love, for I have loved you.*

*I pray for me. Can You pray for me? Yes, I know You can and do. Holy Spirit, I don't even know what to pray, but I know You're listening.*

> God, I want to be known as a woman who's completely in love with You and is a friend of God.

*WOW! I have so much to thank You for. Phillip MacIntosh has been a true friend given by You. You're so nice to me, God. How about Your awesome daughters—Sarah and Natalie—wow—good job, God! Lord, together we will magnify You. I wonder what You're doing with our lives; I know it's good; though.*

*Jeremy Camp—his ministry and future wife, bless them. He's so wonderful, protect him from the attacks on his life and use him to win souls daily. Protect him from the wrong girls so he can receive the beautiful gift of the pure bride You have for him. May his love for You grow deeper and his knowledge of You increase. Provide for him financially so he will be freed to serve You always. Pray for his family, bless them; his sister and his relationship to grow closer. Pray for her husband to love You and her. Pray for their church in Indiana, that You bless Pastor Camp and his wife, to be so effective and eternally blessed! Strengthen them in You! I also pray for Jeremy's younger brothers, Jared and Josh, that they would glean from the wisdom You've put in Jeremy and desire to be men of God, too. Lord, I miss Jeremy, yet I know You've called us apart. Protect him from me. I'm afraid seeing him, I could fall for him, and I don't want and won't ever hurt him again (or be hurt), so protect him from wavering women like me. Wow, You lead odd prayers. Protect me from him as well so I can have eyes to see him as you've desired me to see him; as my faithful brother in You.*

*Pour out Your Spirit upon his life, and shower him with blessings! I believe he's the servant You could be looking for! Amen.*

Easter Sunday arrived, and Melissa was really hurting. She was too sick to go to church; she wanted to stay home and be alone with the Lord.

### Easter Sunday

*Lord Jesus, today is the celebration of Your glorious resurrection, and I'm not at church to celebrate it. I'm sorry for making my health situation worse so that I don't feel well enough to celebrate at church. But I want to praise You here in my room. You did give it all so I might live, so no matter what little pain my life might have, I realize I have life because You gave yours. Glory to Your name. Lord, I need to be humbled before You and praise You. I love You and come before You as Your child in need of help. Oh, Daddy, I wish I could just be caught up in Your arms and fall asleep in Your comfort. I know You're here. Even though my eyes cannot see You, my heart feels You. Jesus, thank You for dying on the cross for my sins, and heavenly Father, thank You for enduring that pain because of Your love for me. I know Your love for me was with You then and is with me now. I love You and desire to praise You in a mighty way. I don't want to have to hide, I want to feel great and be great in Your eyes. Yes, Jesus, I realize by Your blood, I am forgiven, pure, and blameless. Jesus, You are so holy, and I love You so much. Open the eyes of my heart to look upon You in a new way. Jesus, let's change my situation to be Your situation. I know I'll feel better if I put healthier food in my body and if I put Your good in first, always, and last. Jesus, I want to worship You!*

*Jesus, I want to go to church tonight and worship You. Help me change now. Jesus, I need You so much. I need Your wisdom, Your forgiveness, Your love, and Your strength. Jesus, I know You'll give me the strength to endure anything that comes my way. Help me to praise You through this.*

Throughout Easter Sunday, Melissa was focused on worshiping Jesus and her love for Jeremy. She was missing him. She confided in me and her brother Ryan that she loved Jeremy. We were both a little stunned.

Easter Sunday night she was feeling better and was really excited to go to The Rock's open-air service at San Diego State. She left with her sister Megan and friends. Her Dad and I came a little later. As we were walking towards the amphitheater, we could hear music and looked towards the stage and saw Jeremy. We could see Melissa down towards the front, waving at us with a huge smile, and pointing up to the stage. She had so much joy in seeing him. We all sat close to the stage, and I could see his eyes glance towards Melissa. I leaned over to her friend and said, "That man loves my daughter!" It was undeniable the love these two had for each other, even in the midst of their struggle. After the service he came down to her and they spoke a little. I asked if she wanted to tell him that she was having surgery in a week. She seemed hesitant.

After he left, Mark went to find him and have a little talk. He wanted Jeremy to know what was happening with Melissa's health and to let him know how much she cared for him. Jeremy's heart was still very guarded. Mark sensed his reluctance to talk and just said, "Don't give up on her, Jeremy." Mark had watched the two of them fall in love before his eyes. Every Thursday night at his college Bible Study or, as Mark would call it, Melissa's college Bible Study, he could see the undeniable, supernatural connection they had. He loved Jeremy. He had a father's intuition that Jeremy was Melissa's chosen one.

*Dear Lord,*

*Thank You for tonight and the mighty blessings. Today I've realized how much Your love never ends, how Your love has no conditions at all. Almighty Lord, You are amazing, and I'm in awe of You. Thank You for rising from the dead and concealing my sin! Lord, it blows me away how tonight I was saying how I miss Jeremy and there he was, leading worship with The Kry. Lord that was so special to see him up there. I feel so connected to his heart, yet pulled away by who we are. I feel as though his spirit and mine are in love with one another. Jesus, I miss him so much. But I don't even know what to pray or ask, because I'm troubled, or at least have been, and I don't want to cause trouble again. Lord, I wish I could spend time with him as a friend and we could see if it is love that binds us. But I know he said he wouldn't do that. So, Lord, protect my heart. I look at him and just wish I could have him all to myself. I feel as though we never are able to share all we should. Lord, I don't know what to pray, but I pray Your Spirit would pray for me. I do thank you for Jeremy and the joy it brought me to see him tonight. What an awesome Easter celebration.*

*Lord, I feel my heart and ears need to listen to You. I know I've listened to others in the past concerning decisions I'm making, and I want to listen only to You. I trust You have my best interests in mind. So, Lord, I will not ask for a sign, but for wisdom. Grant me discernment and knowledge to know Your will. Lord, grant Jeremy wisdom as well. I know we tend to rely on our feelings to lead and guide, and I pray we would rely on You. Lord, if Jeremy felt moved tonight because of me, I ask he would give it to You. I know his heart fears mine, but I also know You're a huge God and, in Your timing . . . if it were Your will . . . You could heal that. You could restore a new heart in Jeremy and have him look at me in a new way. If You've planned for us to be together and minister together, please put a clear passion in our hearts.*

*Lord, I pray Jean-Luc would help Jeremy see Your will. Jesus, my heart loves the passion Jeremy has. My heart longs for that. My entire being wants to be with him, yet I will not do anything to act on that. I must trust that if You want us together, You will do a miracle. Lord, I love You and I love Jeremy Camp. I do, I love him, help me know if I am the woman I pray for him. Lord, if I'm not to be his wife and it's another young woman You have me praying for, please take away these feelings for him. I desire nothing but blessings in his life. I pray whatever way I am to be involved in his life will be blessings. I pray for his heart to be steadfast and strong in You. Help him know Your will and seek it with all his heart. I pray for the ministry in Huntington, that it would be awesome and You would use his gifts there. Jesus, bless my dear brother and friend Jeremy. Help him focus on You and remember or forget me as You would will it. Give me a comfort in whatever happens in the days to come. Whether he calls or not, allow me to trust and wait upon You.*

*What was I afraid of . . . Loving the wrong man? Why didn't I appreciate him then? I felt it was too fast to know if it was love. What does my heart truly feel? I know I love him deeply, but am not sure if it's love for a husband. What would have to happen for me to know? Peace and joy in my heart and before God that I could run up to his face and say, "I love you," because nothing is worth hurting him again.*

*Lord, please allow him to be my friend.*

*Lord, how can I increase my love in discernment and knowledge?*

*What are the excellent things I can approve? What qualities do I need to pursue to become a woman of excellence?*

*Know God intimately, Melissa!*

*He is your source and model of excellence. Understanding God's love, sovereignty, and provision encourages you to want to reflect His excellence.*

*Melissa, you deceive yourself if you think trying to be perfect will make God accept you more. "But God demonstrates His own love toward us, in that while we were still sinners, Christ died for us" (Romans 5:8).*

*God's love had nothing to do with our love, for He died in the midst of our sin, becoming sin for us. God is so good, and His love never ends.*

> God constantly encourages me to return to His love by living securely in Him. I want to become a woman of excellence, not because I have to perform but because I choose to please God, who loves me completely!

God's power. "Whatever the Lord pleases He does, In heaven and in earth, in the seas and in all deep places" (Psalm 135:6). Lord, do whatever pleases You, for I know You will!

Ruth (2:12) sought refuge under God's wings and "happened" into the field of Boaz, who offered her protection. Because Ruth trusted God with her life, He guided and guarded her. Melissa, remember God's grace is sufficient to triumph through your trials and bear up under them.

> God has charged Himself with the responsibility for our eternal happiness, not our present happiness. Lord God, may I remember the eternal happiness You have for me and that I will live forever with You.

Lord, I am longing to pour out my heart to You and sing to You the longing of my heart. I love You; I need You. You're wonderful, and I'm so thankful for all You've done for me.

Lord, I could worship You on the top of the hills and across the sea. My Lord and Savior, I feel Your eternal love for me. I know this love we share is my eternal happiness that cannot be compared.

Jesus, I'm ready now to be completely Yours in every way I can.

My life, my love, my heart, my soul, You know it's all Yours to control.

Oh Lord, I couldn't be more filled with joy knowing You'll guide and direct my every step. Lord, I look to the ocean and see something new. I feel so overwhelmed with joy, as if I could fly above and across this sea proclaiming Your never-ending love for me. I know my face must be glowing with You, for I feel as though I'm flying now. Jesus, how You love a sinner as wretched as me and take me in Your arms and make me clean. How You bury my pain far away and cleanse me within each new day. How You listen to my heart and words unspoken and answer my prayers in such short time. How Your love reveals Your almighty power. How Your love reveals who You are. Lord Jesus Christ, my risen King, You are my everything. You're the Son of God, the Prince of Peace, everlasting Almighty King. You're my family's God across the nation and my God, so sovereign. You're the joy I see in the faces of believers. You're the love I feel from amongst my friends. You're the one I love inside of Jeremy, and You're the one who's eternally set me free.

*Jesus Christ, my love for all time, I worship You during this life. I can't wait to see Your face and have Your glory revealed to my eyes. I can't wait to hear You call my name and know I'll never leave Your sight.*

*Jesus, remember that time when I read "shout to the mountains, the Lord reigns"? That was so awesome. Remember the time before my last surgery when I felt your knees when I knelt to pray by my bed? I remember it all and know You do, too. You're so mighty, oh precious Lord, I love You. I can't wait to know more of You each new day. I can't wait for new memories to come my way. I can't wait to worship You today and forever. Jesus, I'm Yours, and You are my treasure.*

*Jesus, tonight at Natalie and Sarah's I realized many things. One, I love to talk, and two, how so many of my decisions have been made based on others around me. When I was telling the girls about my past with Jeremy, I felt so much of it was altered by rash decisions and others' opinions. I wish one could change the past—I would have taken it slow and enjoyed it. I would have prayed more and waited more. I would do things with wisdom. O Lord, You know my heart and how much I miss Jeremy. I know You know his heart, too. Lord, there is nothing he or I can hide from You. So, Lord, will You increase my faith to trust in You with our lives? I feel the past is something I can learn from and the future is what I can do my best by seeking You in. I'm glad to see my past was filled with mistakes I can learn from. I've learned to trust my heart's desire and to turn to You first, and You alone. Listen to advice, but trust and obey You! Lord, I love You.*

*Lord, can You give Jeremy and me a vision, the same vision? You know You can, and I ask You would give me one, but I would rely on Your Word to lead and guide me.*

*If I had no fears, I would go to Hawaii this summer and witness to everyone. I would fast and ask Your will. I would pray for Jeremy and me to know Your will. I would return home and pray about Bible College. I would go to Bible College, if the Lord willed. I would commit to loving Jeremy for all my life. I would serve in ministry; I would help his ministry. I would wait until the Lord had done a miracle to restore Jeremy's heart, and I would tell him I love him.*

*Lord, this isn't what I'll do if I have no fear. This is what I'll do if You will.*

*Change Jeremy's heart to see me as You desire him to or change my heart to see him as You desire me to. Or bring us together as You desire. May he feel my prayers reaching out to him tonight. I do pray more than anything that he would mature in knowledge and wisdom of Your Word, but mostly be intimately in love with You. Prepare him for the road of ministry he has ahead of him, and prepare him for his partner. I pray she gives him more love than he could imagine. O, I want to love him; help me know if that's what I shall commit to. Open my eyes through prayer and fasting. Thy will be done.*

*Melissa, one day you'll realize you make decisions based on the wisdom I've given you and passions you have. Recognize that which your heart beats for.*

*Lord, I was going to pray about where I should live and have discovered You know.*

*From one man He made every nation of men, that they should inhabit the whole earth; and He determined the times set for them and the exact places where they should live. God did this so that men would seek Him and perhaps reach out for Him and find Him, though He is not far from each one of us.*

*— (PARAPHRASE OF ACTS 17:26-27)*

*So, Lord, I trust You know where I'll live, and then I'll seek You and find You're near.*

The next night Melissa and her friends went to a Bible Study that Jeremy and his roommates were having. She was so excited to see him again. Lis and J spent some time together talking in his car.

*Tonight, seeing Jeremy and worshiping with him and the group was wonderful. Lord, I thank You for Your amazing love, and I pray that if*

*Jeremy and I are meant to love one another, You would provide me with peace and assurance and provide him with forgiveness and trust toward me through You! I love seeing You in Him! Amen.*

*Today I continue fasting, praying, and mostly seeking Your face. Lord, You're my life, and I love You more than this life You've given me. So, may I draw near to You and know You'll be found. Mighty is the only and true God I serve. I ask You would continue to show me wisdom and love through Your Word and help me see clearly the desires of my heart. I pray that You'd be in control and I would be willing. Prepare me spiritually and physically for the days to come before my surgery and use this to bring You glory. I lift up dear Jeremy to You and ask as I pray and lift him up to You continually that You would do a miracle in his life. I know You'll use him and bless him, thank You. I pray that my love for him would grow if that be in Your will, and that I would cast my fear away and love him. I love You, Lord, and trust that whatever happens will be for our good. Love You, Amen.*

Melissa and I walked down the long hospital corridor towards the radiology department for yet another sonogram. My heart was pounding, but I found peace in my sweet daughter's face. The Lord is good, and I knew He was holding Lis tight. I waited. Melissa came out of the room, and we began walking back down that long hospital corridor. "Mom, something is wrong. I could tell by how the technicians responded and how they were looking at me." I held her tight as we walked back to the car and prayed.

*Jesus, I love You so much and will faithfully praise You in everything. You are my rock, and it's on You I stand. I love Your Word and the peace You give. I love how You are in love with me and have created me to be in love with You. O Lord, I know You patiently wait for me to be prepared for the news to come. O Jesus, I fear the prayer I'm about to pray will be a prayer like the last time You prepared me for the worst. But I will grab hold of my fear and my worries, and I will cast them out of my mind in Your name, Jesus.*

*I trust You with my life. I lay my life down at the cross, and I'll count the cost of my flesh to die as You faithfully reign in me.*

*Lord Jesus, I was alarmed today at the hospital during the ultrasound. I felt I saw something worse than we expected, and now having Dr. Price leave a message concerning it . . . it does worry me.*

*So, Lord, I will wait upon You and know*
*You are preparing me for this journey*
*and that I'll never go through it alone.*

*You know, Lord, the thought of my health being worse than just a cyst makes me realize how much I love Jeremy. Because even though I truly believe I hold a true and pure love for him, I would not be able to give him my heart only to give him bad health. So, I pray if You have created me to love Jeremy, that my love will be selfless. I pray I would hold this love as You hold me until You heal me. Lord, I don't think I would be able . . .*

The oncologist called and explained to me that the sonogram showed Melissa had fluid built up in her abdomen. It could be one of two things—either a leaking cyst or "bad" fluid. Bad fluid would mean cancer. He scheduled surgery immediately.

Melissa was not rattled—she was not moved. Her abdomen was swollen and uncomfortable. She went back to writing. I was numb. It was a feeling that I would become accustomed to. In my room, I cried out to God for my daughter's life.

*OK, the doctor just called, Lord, and I know I'm Yours. I belong to You. So, Jesus, take me as I am and heal me. Do a miracle. Lord, I pray the fluid in my belly wouldn't infect me and hurt my health, and that the cyst wouldn't leak anymore. Give me Your strength. I love You and eternally trust You.*

*I wait for the Lord, my soul waits*
*In His word I place my trust and rest*
*Put a new song in my heart*
*Take away all our fears*

*The Lord is near to all*
*Trust in the Lord with all of your heart. Lean not on your own understanding. In all of your ways acknowledge Him, and He will direct your path.*

*O Lord, my soul thirsts for You and longs for You more and more.*

*After Thursday night (7 a.m.)*

"*I waited patiently for the* LORD; *and He inclined to me, and heard my cry. He also brought me up out of the horrible pit, out of the miry clay, and set my feet upon a rock, and established my steps. He has put a new song in my (heart) mouth—praise to our God; Many will see it and fear, and will trust in the Lord. Blessed is the man who makes the* LORD *his trust.*"

*—*PSALM *40:1-4*

*Oh Lord, I will wait upon You patiently. I have so much to wait for. Precious Jesus, I love how I can tell You anything and everything and You listen. Teach me how to listen to You.*

*Jesus, I love You so! Thank You for this love and strength in the midst of this difficult time. Jesus, I pray for my family. Guard their hearts from lies and give them strength in You. As my mom says, to strengthen ourselves in You. Lord, I lift up Jeremy again. I thank You for allowing him to continually bring me joy as I pray for him. Lord, things come and go, including these young bodies we have, but love lasts forever. Jesus, I want to love Jeremy Camp forever with You. Continue to increase his love and passion for You more and more. O Jesus, today when the news came of my growth leaking, it made me think of how I wanted to stop my feelings. I now realize I can't stop them anymore. The way I feel for Jeremy can't be contained anymore. Jesus, I love him. So, Lord, I pray You would protect my body for him. I desire to get well and share with Jeremy how I love him so. I know Your plan is a great and mighty one, and I'll continue to know this even if I don't get well. Please show me discernment in how and when You want me to share these feelings with Jeremy. Help me continue to keep them between You and me, so it will be all the more special when I give this to him.*

*Jesus, I know You know how everything in me wants to run to Jeremy and embrace him now, apologize for causing my heart to be bland in the past, and let him know You've made me see. I long to tell him how I believe with all my heart that You, our precious Lord, have created our hearts for one another. I know I was lying when I said I believe You've called us to different ministries, because all I want to do is come alongside his and support him. Jesus, grab hold of my heart, for it pounds for Jeremy right after it beats for You. Now, I can share this with You because I know I need not hold anything back from You.*

*Lord, I've come to the possibility that my life may be shortened, and if it is, I thank You now for this beautiful love You've given me—first for You, my true first love, and second for Jeremy, the one I love with You. Jesus, I ask that my love for him would see Your will and what is best for him. I wouldn't want to take his love if You would take my life. I pray Jeremy and I could trust You with our hearts. Help him let it go, help him see Your will for him and me. But most of all, bless him first. I believe he and I would make a beautiful couple who would love You and each other forever. I see us ministering together and even having our own family together. Jesus, thank You! Thank You for making my love for You and for Jeremy continually increase. You are so awesome. I can't wait to release this love, not only toward You but to Jeremy. Lord, thank You for the new song You have put in my mouth. And no matter what the future, help me see Your will through Your eyes. I desire You to be glorified.*

*Father, I pray for the lost souls at Carlsbad on Saturday, that this group would see them and help reach them where they're at and bring them to You. Your Word is the power unto salvation. I pray that Jeremy and I will feel comfortable around each other and that You would take away awkward feelings his heart holds towards me and show him our love. Amen.*

*Oh, Jesus my love, good morning! I forgot to tell You our little reminder last night; so, let me tell You now. Jesus, I love You more today than yesterday. Help me love You more tomorrow, too! Fill me with Your love this morning so I may know You well. Lord, my heart burns to know You more. My life longs for each new moment You give it, simply to glorify You. Jesus, my love for You is so vast that my words don't know how to declare it. I love that You see in my heart and know my love for You, Jesus.*

*I praise You for this trial upon my body. I know You have taken what the world would say is awful and turned it into something beautiful. Almighty Lord, I love You, and this love is worth any physical pain. Your grace, Your mercy, Your forgiveness, Your never-ending love makes all my little trials seem trivial.*

*The love You had for me caused You, my Lord, to die for me. How grateful my heart is to be able to praise You and thank You. Jesus, lover of my soul, thank You for making it possible for me to love You and know You. O my Lord, You are so good to me. I feel so blessed and special, because here I am embraced in Your arms of love, and it's the best place I've ever been. How true You are, and how my soul just can't stop worshiping You with song. Jesus, Name above all names, King of kings and Lord of lords, Prince of Peace, Friend, Savior, God Almighty, Abba Father, I love You. Touch my body and cause Your love to permeate through me. I feel You now more than ever and long to know You more and more. You say if anyone lacks wisdom, let him ask of God, who gives liberally to all without finding fault, and it will be given him (James 1:5). Jesus, I lack wisdom, and I pray I would be given understanding as I read Your Word. I desire to know You deeply and intimately. I see what a sinner I am and how unrighteous I can be, and yet I see myself as white as snow through Your blood. I love You and give You everything. This life I live is Yours, so do with me as You desire—I'm Yours!*

*Lord, I pray for Heather and ask You would prepare the way for her to be able to be here on Monday. I can't believe I'm going in for surgery at 8:00 a.m. Monday morning.*

*I ♡ U! ☺ Lord, You know it's so awesome, the love I have with You, because it makes me see things Your way. I was thinking of Jeremy and realize that even though I love him deeply, if he couldn't ever love me again or I end up being too inflicted to share my love, Your love was worth living for and You have been the lover of my soul. Jesus, my love for Jeremy is only an offspring of Your love. So I can be more than content with whatever happens to us, knowing I hold Your amazing love in my heart and it's more than enough for me!*

*Dear Lord, I know You're also doctor, so I pray Your wisdom and guidance would be upon Dr. Koonings the GYN oncologist (cancer man) and Dr. Price my surgeon. I know You'll use them to bring me through, if it's even Your will for me to have this surgery.*

*Lord, I'm willing for You to work in me
however You desire. Whether to heal me now,
later, or in heaven, it's all good to me.
I'm so glad I have Your love and peace
to bring me through this.*

*I pray You would use this in my doctors' lives to show them how Jesus in me can make the world of difference. God, You are so good and so worthy to be praised. I'm so blessed to know and love You. I pray that if my doctors aren't saved, You would use this to bring them to desire and receive salvation. I pray my nurses and even the anesthesiologist—*

*everyone involved—would see Your mighty hand watching over me and my family. Lord, I pray for the waiting room. I pray for You to pour out Your love, mercy, peace, joy, and comfort on them. Bring all those who come to be with us into a time of worship and praise.*

*I thank You so much that this is going to be a beautiful time. I thank You now that this is a beautiful experience. But, Lord, even more than an experience, I pray this would be an awakening. Allow me to see my sin and be humble and broken. I know just because I feel and see Your love enwrapping me, doesn't mean I don't have things to learn from others. I know my strength and peace is all from You, and I claim none of it on my own. All I did was seek You when You may be found, which is now and always for me!*

*I ♡ U!*
*Oh Lord, I can praise You always. I just saw the beautiful card Melissa (Herman) gave me with the precious little girl on her knees praying beside her bed, and I felt my little girl will do the same. I have faith You can heal my womb and protect me and bless me one day with children I may raise to worship and love You. No matter if my womb is barren or blessed, I will help bring children into a deep love and adoration for You. Lord, I pray You would give me the strength and wisdom to let the girl disciples know what's going on and how You are with me. I'm sorry for focusing on myself, my discomfort or situation, and putting them after me. I want to be less selfish and more Christ-seeking. Help me be selfless. Amen.*

*I praise the Lord for today*
*For He's made me see you in a new way*
*First it began through complete surrender*
*And then it grew through fasting and prayer*
*The Lord revealed my bondage and fear*
*And has made me see who I long to be near*
*My heart has been waiting for this very day*
*Longing to tell you these words I will say*
*But before I do, I must tell you this—*
*The words you'll hear are my faithful promise*
*Before I could tell you what I'll now say,*
*You need to know it's Jesus who brought me here today*
*Jeremy Camp, I love you*
*Already to hear how I can now see*
*How the Lord graciously removed the fear that blinded me.*
*The Lord is so good and gracious and kind*
*So faithful and loving, too,*
*To think He's created us to love*
*It causes you to see Him in heaven above*
*I praise You, Lord, for Your never-ending love*
*I praise You for the strength You give to the weak*
*I praise You for the gift to worship Your holy name*
*I praise You for life and all the trials the same*
*I magnify Your name because it's above all other names*
*I magnify Your Word, for it is the power unto salvation.*
*I magnify Your might, for You are might, Jesus.*
*I ♡ U!*
*How blinded I was*
*By fear*
*And He's taking it away*
*And now I see clear*

*If I could tell Jeremy whatever is on my heart, and it would be blessed by*
*God and forever bless his life, that is what would I say.*
*"Lord, show me what's in my heart to say to him." Amen.*

*Jeremy, Every time I see your face, my heart beats with joy. But every* time I'm also reminded of the pain I caused you to go through. Do you know every day I wished I could take that back, knowing how awful that must have been? And now I know it could have all been prevented. I need to sincerely apologize for being rash with the delicate decision of your heart. I was torn because of my flesh and blinded by my fear, and that caused me to be out of your life for half a year. But every day, and each time I heard or thought of you, I realized my feelings hadn't gone away and still are strong to this day. But they are different than before. Now I know how I feel, and I believe the Lord has shown me what I felt all along. I felt for you because I care for you and wanted to tell you so. But I knew the only way I could ever let you know was if the Lord confirmed it in my heart. So, sweetie, after praying, fasting, and waiting on the Lord, He's shown me.

Lord, as You can see, I just can't wait to tell Jeremy of our fate, so if it's Your will, allow it to come to be and let us love one another forever and through all eternity. Hold my heart in Your hands and allow me to see Your perfect plan. I trust You will give me that song to share when You and I are finished with our fasting and prayer. So, it's in You I give my poems and songs, waiting upon You all the day long. You are my love and Lord of my life, so I joyfully surrender it all to You. I love You, Lord. Amen.

Morning Lord, It's Saturday—tomorrow is Sunday and then my healing begins unless it's already begun, I love You!

Lord Jesus, I pray for Jeremy today, that he would seek You and be willing to hear what You have to share with him. I pray his spirit of fear toward me would be removed and he would be free to see Your will for him and me. Thank You for allowing me to bless him in prayer before I'm able to share with him. I love You, Lord. Your will be done! Amen.

*Friends and family,*
*Do you know how happy I am now? The joy in my heart can't be expressed,*
*but I need to write it down.*

> Jesus, my love, our Lord, our Savior and King, has fulfilled my life completely. No matter what small or large pain I go through or will, I will praise Christ. His love and His plan are so good, and all we are called to do is trust it. No matter what we think we need to remember, our home is in heaven with Jesus our God, so whatever happens as we pass through Earth, make sure it glorifies God so you can have the joy of His love even before your eyes see His face.

*Lord, loving You is the greatest gift I've ever experienced.*

*Jesus, the pain my body bears now
I bear proudly, knowing You endured
so much more pain because of Your
love for me. So how may I bear this
pain for You? I praise You and
glorify You through this.*

*I love You. I trust You and need you! I want You! I feel You! Thank You Lord, Amen.*

*I also pray that Jeremy and I would be in Your will and Your timing. I love him, Lord, and wish I may have a healthy physical body to love him with. So, I pray if he will (or does) love me too, that our faith in You will be our health, our strength, and the source of our love forever! Amen. Continue to work in my heart. Show me boldness and how to use everything to bring You glory! Be now magnified!*

*Oh Lord, Heather just called, and how amazing that Mr. Post offered to fly her home Sunday. I pray that would be a huge blessing, and that she would be completely protected by Your angels guiding her home.*

*Lord, I pray for Jeremy, that You would bless him today with a pure desire for You. I pray his heart would desire Your will completely for his life, no matter what that may be. I pray his music would continue to be anointed, and that You would bless it and all those who hear it. I pray that his spiritual gifts would provide financially for him all the days of his life. Lord, I pray his family would feel a burden on their heart to pray for Jeremy and me, and that You would open his eyes to see the love You have given me for him.*

Melissa spent the Saturday before her surgery doing one of her favorite things: she met with a group of Christians that she dearly loved down in Carlsbad. It was a habit of theirs to go witnessing every Saturday. Then, that night we all went to Saturday night service at Horizon Christian Fellowship. She then spent the evening writing.

*Saturday*

*Lord, thank You for today. Thank You for the privilege to witness down in Carlsbad today to Paul, the little old man. I pray that the words and Scripture Sarah, Natalie, and I shared would be remembered in his heart. I pray the Word we gave him would be read and You would bless it. I pray he would remember what we shared and share it with his wife. I also pray for Leo the homeless man. I ask the Words and love we gave would help direct him to cry out to You and believe in You. I pray also for the man at the bus stop that Sarah talked with. I pray he would remember the words she shared and not remember Sarah, but You, Jesus! I pray he would desire You and seek and find You. Jesus, I thank You for today and for Tyler and Chris, Megan and Sam, Natalie, Sarah, and me. I thank You for the privilege You've given us to be faithful to You.*

*Satan is so small, and You are so big. I will praise You forever and ever. I love You, Lord, with all my heart, and I thank You for giving us all the Holy Spirit so we have the power to witness to others. You are so worthy to be praised. Jesus, all day was sweet, every moment. I thank You for Sarah and Natalie's continual giving spirit that blesses me upon blessings. I thank You mostly for the love they give. Lord, I praise You for tonight and the wonderful Word and worship You gave through Pastor Mike MacIntosh. I needed to worship You tonight in brokenness, adoration, and praise. So, thank You for that gift. Thank You also for Phillip and Pastor Mickey praying for me and anointing me. You're a mighty God, and we have peace trusting in You. I know my body belongs to You, so it's my privilege to glorify You through it.*

*Family/friends letter:*
*1 Corinthians 6:19-20*
*Through this gift I've been given, the Lord has blessed my life. The Lord has shown me His faithful commitment to love me forever. Many of you thought I was so strong, and yet so many times I was so weak. In fact, I tried handling this life's situation on my own, and that led to carnality for about a week. Now I know no one is above falling away from the love of the Lord. But what began as a time apart from God turned into the most beautiful time with Him. If you remember how blessed I was the last time I went through surgery, you'll be blown away by what's come of this.*

> *The gracious hand of God has chosen me to go through this pain but for a short while. And what little pain it is when compared to the immeasurable love in my heart.*

*You know that our Lord's love is so great. So together, as we are rooted and grounded in love, we may be able to understand with each other what is the width and length and depth and height, to know the love of Christ which passes knowledge; that we all may be filled with all the fullness of God (Ephesians 3:17-19).*

*I looked back on the past and saw how close the Lord was near to me when I went through surgery last September. I thought, "If only I could be that close to the Lord again." I know now how I underestimated God. The love and comfort I experienced then was only the beginning of forever. Jesus has taught me that each new day, each new moment, is a moment to love Him more. God's love is over us like a banner, and it's revealed to us the more we open our eyes and look up. Before I knew what I was facing, I was blind. Blinded by fear to see all the Almighty Lord has in store for me. Now through His love, I can see now His perfect plan.*

Lord, tonight I sleep to awake to Monday! Yay! We are gonna get this sucker out, unless You, Dr. God, have gotten it out already. So, I pray You'd prepare my heart and my family to praise You now and tomorrow through this. Help me deny my flesh and count this little pain I'm privileged to bear to praise You through. Help me minister to all and all to be ministered to. Reign in us and bring us closer to You. May salvation be stunned in the dead because of the believers. Amen! Have Your will, and I pray for peace.

"Do not fear any of those things which you are about to suffer . . . and you will have tribulation. . . . Be faithful until death, and I will give you the crown of life."

—REVELATION 2:10

Good Morning!
I want you all to know that I've been thinking about you and praying for you.

> *I know the Lord has allowed this growth in my flesh to cause a growth in my spirit, and yet this is not only for me.*

*My love and happiness for the Lord has never been greater, and yet I know it will continue to grow by His grace. So, as you wait upon the Lord to see what His perfect and good will is for me, I pray you all can praise the Lord! No matter what happens today, the outcome will be great.*

> So, let's all come together and praise the Lord for this and look for every opportunity given to bring glory to His Holy Name. Let's grow in faith, hope, and love. I love you all, and remember whose mighty hands I'm resting in! Ephesians 3:16-19.

*Love you, Melissa*

# CHAPTER

## 4

## ALL HIS WAYS ARE GOOD AND KIND

*W*e arrive at the hospital early Monday morning, May 1, for surgery prep. Melissa has great peace and has written us a letter and a prayer.

*Dear family and everyone,*
*I love you all so very much and can't imagine what you are going through together. So, I would love to pray for you as you wait to see what the gracious Lord has in store for me. So, let's worship the Lord and magnify His name together!*

> *Heavenly Father, we come before You with grateful hearts, praising You for the mighty works You do. Lord Jesus, giver of all good things, we praise You for allowing this to happen to me. Father in heaven and Lord of my life, we will continue to praise You all the day long. I simply ask for You to be with all those whose ears this prayer falls upon. I pray asking that the almighty love and peace and joy that has been poured out upon me will be poured out upon all of these children. Lord, as I rest in Your arms trusting my life to You, I pray that Your goodness will see my whole family through. Take all of their fears and graciously dry any tears so all will see how faithful You are. We lean not on our own understanding, but on the promises in Your Word. So, bring this body of believers together to worship You and eat Your Word. I'm praising You now, not in my strength, but solely in the strength You have given. So, lover of my soul, we give You our lives to Your control and our hearts' emotions to praise Your name. Almighty God, Prince of Peace! Abba Father, Lord of our lives! You are so worthy to be praised, and we pray to worship You until the day we can worship You face-to-face. We love You, Lord, and trust all of our lives to be in Your hands. Thank You for right now, thank You for choosing us to*

*be a family together, and give us eyes to see those searching for You, their Father! I love You, Lord, and praise Your name. May Your will be done in everyone here and in me. Amen.*

Melissa is prepped for surgery. Her Dad and I pray with her. Dr. Price and Dr. Koonings come into her room. Melissa smiles at them and asks if they will pray with her. She reaches out her hands to hold theirs and then prays for them. Our precious girl is not worried. She has no fear, only peace. Her concerns are for her family, her friends, and her doctors. She prays for them to have wisdom and prays for them to trust the Lord. I am in awe.

Her family and friends are gathered in the waiting room. I pace up and down the corridor. I pace and pray. There are huge windows between the surgery doors and the waiting room that look out over the parking lot to a church with a cross boldly standing above the building. I stop pacing and gaze upon the cross, remember Christ's suffering for us and the Scriptures that tell me that we can know not just the power of His resurrection, but also the fellowship of His suffering.

My mind can't handle the thought of my child suffering—I want to take it from her and put it upon myself. That's what Jesus did for us. He will carry Melissa through; He will carry me through. We visit the chapel next door to the waiting room and pray and wait. The surgery is long. I continue to pace back and forth down the corridor between the waiting room and surgery doors. It is suffocating.

I observe many families waiting for news of their loved ones. Doctors appear in front of the waiting room and call out their names. They meet a doctor in the corridor, and we can see the joy on their faces when they hear the good news that the surgery went well, and all is fine. Relief and joy were so evident on their faces.

After about five hours, a door opens in the back of the waiting room. Dr. Koonings appears and calls out, "Henning." *Why isn't he calling us from the front corridor?* We all get up and go back to a little room with him, and he closes the door. We sit down; he sits down. He proceeds to tell us that Melissa has cancer and that it has spread from her ovary to her intestines and liver. He says he removed all that he could and removed her ovary but left the rest of her reproductive organs intact. It is stage 3C ovarian cancer.
This room was the bad news room.

The only explanation I have for my response is that the Holy Spirit took over. My daughters Heather and Megan were crying and burying their heads in my lap. I stroked their hair and just kept saying over and over through my soft tears, "All God's ways are good and kind, All God's ways are good and kind." Heather kept crying, "No, no, don't do this!" Needless to say, we were devastated. Ryan rushed out of the room, and I later found out he just couldn't breathe and went outside and punched a wall. He was distraught and beyond consoling. Mark quietly got up and met with the doctor outside of the room to get as much information as he could. The girls and I sat in the bad news room for a long time, crying. I couldn't feel my body. I was numb all over. In the midst of the worst news, the only thing I could feel was the comfort of the Holy Spirt and the assurance that all God's ways are good and kind.

Nurses brought Melissa out of recovery to her room. Dr. Koonings told me she wouldn't wake up until about 4 in the morning, and that I would be the one to tell her she had cancer. "Oh, Lord, how do I do that? How do I tell my beautiful twenty-year-old daughter she has cancer?" I struggled to breathe. Heather and I stayed the night in her room and slept on the floor next to her bed, mom on one side and big sister on the other. I didn't sleep all night. I could not stop weeping. Heather kept encouraging me to stop; she didn't want Melissa to wake up and hear me crying. I prayed and asked for strength and wisdom to know what to say and how to say it. I couldn't formulate a thought. I couldn't come up with the right words.

Melissa began to wake up. Her first words were, "Mom! How's Miles? Mom, are you fasting for Miles?"
"Yes honey, Miles is fine and yes, I am fasting."
She seemed relieved and fell back to sleep.
"Mom, I don't want to know the news yet, but how was the news for you, are you OK? Is everyone alright?"
"Yes, honey, I'm OK, we're all OK."
She fell peacefully back to sleep.
A couple of hours later, "Mom, I'm ready to hear the news." She ran her fingers down her abdomen and gently asked. "Was it the good fluid or the bad fluid?"
"The bad fluid, honey."
"Is it cancer?"
"Yes, honey."
She literally was glowing and said, "Oh, Mom! That is so great, God is going to do such amazing things." Pause . . . then, with even more excitement, "The Stones are going to get saved!"

All His ways are good and kind. He walked us gently through the "news." I had no need to worry about the words I would say; the Lord had already prepared the conversation. It was beautiful.

Melissa's response stunned us. Her first thought was not for herself, but for a pastor who was having throat surgery at the same time. Together we had been praying for him, pleading with the Lord to save his voice so he could continue to preach the Word of God. It brought a sweet smile to Melissa's face knowing that Miles McPherson's voice was spared that day. Secondly, she was concerned for me, her mother. I was and still am humbled by the love she had and has for me. She was concerned for me, and how I was with the news, and if everyone was alright. There was not one thought about herself. **I was stunned and in awe, but even more stunned by her reaction to the news that it was cancer.**

> *Oh, Mom! That is so great, God is going to do such amazing things! . . . The Stones are going to get saved!*

Who does that? The faith of my child was challenging mine, pushing mine, increasing mine. I was transported from despair to hope—great hope. Melissa knew her God. She knew He loved her supremely, and He would not ask her to go through cancer without a great, amazing plan to show off His handiwork. She knew her life existed for His purposes and His plans to draw people to Himself—to show off His grace, His mercy, His forgiveness, and to reveal Himself and His glory through her. She said with awe and humility,

> *Oh, that God would consider me worthy to go through this.*

She actually considered it an honor for God to have chosen her for this path of suffering, with the confidence others would come to know Jesus through it. Her mind and heart immediately focused on the Stones.

The Stones are our neighbors, and Melissa had known them most of her life. She loved them all very much, and they loved her. Her heart turned to them with the confidence that God would use this in her life to bring them to faith in Jesus.

> *Lord Jesus, I will wait for You. My soul shall wait. In Your precious Word I'll trust, and in Your mighty Word I'll rest, for I know I must wait. Jesus, I understand that this battle I am fighting isn't my own, but it's Yours. And I know any battle You fight is a victorious one. Precious Lord, I thank You that You are the One who gives me hope and healing. Lord, I am going to come running to You for Love, for help, and for healing. I want to grow closer to You moment by moment.*

> *I know that there is a spiritual war going on for me, against the work You and I are going to do. But I will fight and get my strength from You.*

> *I will press on and continue to wait for healing to be more and more evident in my life. Please comfort me with Your healing hands and prepare me for the humbling and brokenness You still have in store for me. O, Mighty Lord whom I love, have Your way in me.*

# CHAPTER

## 5

## If One Life ...

The word began to spread to Melissa's friends and so many people who loved her. The halls began to fill with people praying for her outside of her room. Doctors, nurses, and techs were in and out of her room every few minutes. You could tell which ones were just doing their job and staying detached from this beautiful young woman with cancer. Then, there were others who seemed like they were gifts from God—angels unaware. They had compassion and concern and cared for her as I would. Really, as Jesus would. I became convinced that angels walked the halls of that hospital and entered Melissa's room with God's special touch.

Some friends knew Melissa loved red and yellow roses. They brought a huge bouquet of them to her room. One of the emotionally detached nurses came into her room to take her vitals and record the data. She looked away from Melissa the whole time and never engaged with her.

Sweet Melissa said to her, "Thank you so much for caring for me." Stunned, the nurse didn't know what to say. Then Melissa said, "Mom, please give her a rose." I asked her what color she would like, and gladly gave her one in that color. Melissa again thanked her as she was leaving with her rose. When she was awake, every nurse, doctor, or technician who entered her room, male or female, was thanked by her and given a rose. The countenance of those who were detached changed. They began to see her, talk to her, and listen to her. They loved her. Some became like mother bears, protecting her with fierceness. They would shoo people out of her room so she could sleep and even changed the location of her room to a more private, back corner room away from the crowds that would gather to pray. They were determined to do everything possible to help our sweet girl recover. It was evident there was something different, special, even supernatural about Melissa.

*I ask that my life will be praising and pleasing to You and Your name. I want my life to be a beautiful reflection of how Your love to me is. I want to serve You, Father, as You have served me.*

*In Hawaii, I realize a lot of my true nature. I realize the love and compassion I have. So much love for my family. I desire my family to be close, and I always realize that when I am in Hawaii. Another thing I realize is how human I am. If I do not concentrate on being a servant for God I will, minute by minute, fail Him. But I also have realized that my love for God does not cease. It does not stop because I am happy or sad. My moods have nothing to do with my salvation. (Thank You, God, because I would be condemned to hell if it were so!) I also realize that God is merciful and gracious. We take it for granted. I take it for granted. His love, yes, it's there, His forgiveness, oh it's there as well, His reasoning. Why God loves me, I can never humanly understand. Why He forgives me, I cannot understand either.*

*I am thinking of a child, and how they are always getting into things and doing the wrong things, and yet they are so wonderful, we love them so much. We forgive them the very moment they say sorry. Even just with the look of their eyes we forgive them. Parents and loved ones of children know facial expressions that say I'm sorry or I'm not, or I'm happy or sad. I think all of this relates to how Jesus Christ, our heavenly Father, knows us. He looks at us and knows our facial expressions, He knows when we are sorry and when we need His love. I think that's why it is so important to be like a child, so we can come to our heavenly Father who lives in us and pray and be forgiven, be loved, changed, grow, and receive all He has in store for us. So many things He has planned for us. I feel it in my heart because He tells me in the Word.*

After Melissa's surgery, Jeremy got a phone call from a good friend, Mike O. Mike was trying to tell him about Melissa, but was struggling with the right words to say. He was beating around the bush and stumbling over his words so much that Jeremy thought Melissa had died in surgery. Mike finally said, "No, she has cancer."

I went and sat out in the main hallway and let others go in Melissa's room to see her. I kept seeing hospital staff coming down the hallway with either a red or yellow rose. I would say to them, "Oh, you've seen Melissa. Thank you." They would always smile. Melissa was a servant of God, an encourager, and a comfort to those who were hurting. Every person who came out of that room was touched by her. Now it was Jeremy's turn.

When Jeremy arrived at the hospital, we asked everyone to leave her room so he could be alone with her. This was their time. Lis was delighted to see him. He stayed with her for quite a while. She always loved talking to him. The conversation was a life changer for Jeremy. She continued to stun with her responses. She told him,

"If one life comes to know Jesus Christ as their Savior because of what I go through, it will be worth it."

One thing was always on her mind: her life's purpose was to glorify God and to lead people to Jesus. Her suffering was insignificant to her. Her focus was on the one life that could be changed for eternity.

Melissa was so excited Jeremy came and adored seeing him. It was obviously very hard on him. He came out into the hallway where I was sitting. I asked him if he was OK, and we had a long talk. I shared with him Melissa's strength and her responses to the news. I also shared with him the song that was ministering to her, the words to Ginny Owens's song "If You Want Me To." She had been giving the words away to everyone. I repeated the line,

> "I will go through the valley
> if You want me to."

Jeremy had to leave to go up to Huntington Beach to lead worship at Calvary Chapel that night. As he was driving, he listened to Ginny Owens's song. He began to weep all the way to Huntington Beach, a good hour's drive away. He cried out to the Lord, knowing this song was the prayer of Melissa's heart.

*"Lord, if You want me to marry her,*
*she has to tell me that she loves me."*

*I pray that no matter what I feel, happy or sad, no matter if I'm lonely or satisfied, I pray throughout it all I may live my life for You. I love You above anything and anyone. You know this to be true. My Jesus, I see my future being an awesome testimony for Your glory. That to me is worth all the loneliness of my day today and forever. I mean by that, if I should never marry, it is worth it, for You. But Jesus, I would love to fall in love with a man that has a heart to serve You as I do. I would love to be united with a man so that together we may increase the work of our Lord Jesus.*

*I am sure of this, that the only way I would marry a man is if You, Lord, brought us together in a miraculous way. The miracle would be in his heart and soul—a man who loves You more than anything and especially more than me.*

Jeremy did not come back to the hospital like we all thought he would. Melissa came home. Dear friends had come and prepared her room for her and freshened up the house. They had bought her a present, and she was delighted. It was a full-length black satin nightgown and robe from Victoria's Secret—modest and beautiful, just like Melissa. She was full of joy. Day after day, many of her friends would come and sit by her bedside. I could hear her talking and laughing as she was doing what she loved—ministering to and comforting others.

Late one night while I was washing the dishes, I heard a tap, tap, tap on the front door. It was Jeremy. All the weird awkwardness of the last six months was gone. He gave me a big hug, and I rushed up to Melissa's room. She was still awake. She had on her new Victoria's Secret nightgown and robe and quickly freshened up. She looked beautiful, not sick—gorgeous, in fact! They laughed and talked for hours in her room. They loved to laugh, and hearing it brought great joy to me and Mark. That night lifted our heavy hearts and gave us our first experience of rejoicing in the midst of our sorrow, fears, and great concern for our daughter's life.

*May 8, 2000*

> *Dear Sweet Jesus,*
>
> *Wow! You're so amazing, and I love You so so much! I'm in absolute awe of how incredible You are, Lord. I'm in awe of Your love; I'm in awe of Your power. I'm in awe of how good You are to me! Lord, You know I love to tell You all my feelings, all my thoughts and cares, and guess what, I'm about*

*to do that. OK, Lord, thank You so much for last night. Last night was so amazingly beautiful and rad. When Ashley and I were lying down in bed and mom came in my room, I couldn't have heard better news. Lord, I'm so excited Jeremy came over. It's so neat looking back on the day and seeing how You had the night so perfect leading up to his coming over. I love how Natalie said she wanted him to see me in my beautiful PJ's, and how I was going to change but decided not to. I love that I told Ashley how I wasn't worried at all, and that I had a peace about him knowing that You, Lord, were doing a work in his heart and mine as well, and if You were showing me something (that I'm in love with him), You could be showing him, Jesus. You're faithful. I know Your sweet, soft voice now. I hear You and know it's You telling me yes to my questions about Jeremy.*

*Jesus, I also believe it's You, the love of my soul, who has the power and hopefully will to heal my body and prepare me for a lifetime of loving Jeremy. Actually, Lord, I know that I will love him for my whole lifetime. I just pray it's a long one. I can't wait for the day he knows I'm deeply, madly, wonderfully in love with him. I can't wait, Jesus, but I faithfully will. I'll wait until You reveal to me it's time to tell him. Jesus, I want to tell him now. I pray he would feel led by You to call me tomorrow to see how things went and that if it be Your will, You'd work it out for us to see one another and talk and pray about all of this. I do pray for Your patience so I can continue to wait upon Your perfect timing. I'm Yours Lord, and at Your call.*

*Thank You for this joy that comes from the released fear and the ability to see Your deep love for Jeremy. Lord, please, by faith I pray Your mighty healing hand would heal my body for Jeremy to have and hold and minister to and with 'til death do us part. Whatever it takes, I will love You, and whatever it takes I will love him for all my life. Thank You for this gift! Every good and perfect gift does come down from You, Father of lights, and it does have no variation or shadow of turning. Lord, life with You is so precious, and loving You is so incredible. Loving You is the greatest joy my life could ever have. Enjoying this banner of love over me is a gift I'll enjoy for eternity, and this gift alone is better than anything else. Even the thought of loving Jeremy for my life is so far above anything I could have imagined. That's a double portion of the love that I know I don't deserve, but would so willingly grab at the chance to have. I love that I'm in Your hands, Lord, and that Your will for my life will bring You glory! I ♡ it! I ♡ U!*

*Lord, speak to me and through me. Help me not fear but believe.*

*I do trust and love You, so whatever Your will is for my life I willingly accept, knowing it will bring glory and honor to Your Holy Name and knowing many will praise You because of the love You have for me.*

*You're so amazing, Lord. I ♡ U! Heavenly Father, speak to Jeremy as well. Reveal my love for him to him in Your perfect timing. I pray Jean-Luc will have wisdom from above when counseling him as a brother, that they together will see Your will. You're awesome, God, and I trust my life, my love, and my everything to You! With all my love for all my life I pray this as I praise my Love, Jesus. Amen.*

Melissa told me the next morning that she was able to ask Jeremy to forgive her for hurting him and to tell him all the things she wanted to—except "I love you." She couldn't do that knowing she had cancer. How could she hurt him? What a night.

# CHAPTER

## 6

# I LOVE YOU

*M*elissa picked up her journal and started writing. This great love she felt inside of her was intensifying, and it poured out of her in prayers for Jeremy. Melissa's heart held an expanse of love from God, and it just exploded all over the pages of her journals. It's like the floodgates were opened, and this love began to cover the whole earth. Well, not exactly, but it felt like that!

Melissa was convinced of her love, and now of her need to tell Jeremy she loved him. She was compelled to tell him. "Mom, I have to tell him I love him." Something changed in her. She no longer feared telling him while she had cancer—that concern just disappeared overnight. I was the one who was concerned, but I never expressed a single doubt to her. I knew God was doing something amazing, and I was just a spectator watching Him work.

*May 11, 2000*

> *Sweet heavenly Father, how precious You are, and how deeply I love You. It's so amazing, because I know that the love I have for other believers is because of the love I have for You! I see love in them that could only come from You, and I recognize it as that. Jesus, You're amazing! What amazing love You have for me and all Your children. You are my King, and I know You'll continually watch out for me. Lord, You know my heart, how much I like what You've done and are doing in my heart.*

> *Dear sweet Lord, I love You so very much and am so grateful that You have been spoiling me with Your Almighty love! The way You have made me feel lately is so extremely blessed and loved and happy and excited. You're just so amazing. I love You!*

*Lord God, tonight I learned You've searched for me. That's beautiful, and I am willing to go through anything—You know it!*

*Jesus, Your love is better than anything, and it makes me shout for joy because of how amazing and almighty it is. Lord, like I feel I need to get away and gather my thoughts now and meditate on You.*

*Hi Jesus, my sweet Jesus! I love You so much and am so blessed to be chosen and loved by You. How can my heart ever express the gratitude Your love brings my life? Lord, You're amazing, and I am in awe of Your majesty and Your kindness. You make life so fun and worth living. You are the reason I move; You are the reason I breathe; You are the reason I live; You are the reason—it's You! And I know that after everything is over, it's over, and You'll be the song I sing forever and ever. "Lord, our Lord, how majestic is your name in all the earth! You have set your glory in the heavens."—Psalm 8:1 (NIV). I will praise You, Lord. I will sing of Your love. I will see Your glory here. Hallelujah, hallelujah, praise the Lord.*

*Jesus, today I lie here on my bed smiling from ear to ear. This joy upon my face has been given by Your grace. Your love is so intense that my arms could never fully grasp it, but my face will surely shine with my Jesus countenance. Your faithfulness continually blesses my soul with the promises of Your Word that I have and dearly hold. You've blessed me with a relationship no marriage or man could ever bring, for my promise to be pure to You has brought me everything. I know my works are merely the result of the power of Your hand. And Jesus, it's only by this grace that You've enabled me to stand. It's funny how the other day I was asked by a Christian brother a question I would have never thought I could answer wrong, Lord. He asked me if I was depressed, and it was only then that I could see. This lost world would take this trial and deal with it wrongfully. So, I praise You, Jesus, for the answer my Spirit shouted out, for I never thought nor will again that I could feel that way. Thank You, Jesus, for Your love that won't allow deep sadness; thank You for Your Love that gives me continual gladness.*

*Jesus, I have prayed to You over the years and have asked many things, so it's now I ask my deepest desire and pray You'd grant it to me. Lord, willingness and flexibility is how I want to live. By Your grace and mercy, even when I can't comprehend, I know this cancer You've allowed has gifted me in many ways, and because of that I know my life will never be the same. O Lord, I pray that I may be continually faithful to You, that even if my deep request never is followed through, I pray even before I ask, that my heart would not fall apart so I may be Your willing and perfectly able child. Sweet Jesus, Your grace has given me eyes to see not only a new way, but where my heart longs to be. Jesus, Lord and my love, maker and father, too, it's also Your deep love that has given me eyes for two. I see You with a deeper love than I ever saw before. I feel Your abundant love, and I'm completely and more abundantly satisfied, but what I will now say I can no longer keep inside.*

*O, sweet Jesus, You know that my heart loves another, too. But it will always first be in love with You. Jesus, these past months and weeks I've realized something new, and it's my heart for Jeremy, that I believe has come from You. I love him so very much, and it's a miracle I know, for last September I was sure I'd forever let him go. How blessed am I to have a heart deeply in love with my Lord and then right underneath in love with Jeremy, who loves You, too. It's his heart that I first fell for, and now can't live without, so Jesus my Almighty God, please take away all my doubt. It's only when I think of him that sorrow fills my heart, for I truly never want him to ever lose me again. Lord, I feel so selfish for loving him now, even when I'm sick inside, but it's a love I know You do not want me to hide.*

*When Jeremy came over Sunday night, exactly one week ago today, I definitely knew that You had answered my prayers. You have put it in my heart to continue to wait and pray, and it's only by Your strength that I'm still doing that today. So, Lord who granted miracles from the beginning of time, I ask You to hear my prayer and grant this one of mine. Take me through this trial of chemotherapy, too, but Lord, I ask most of all You to heal me for You-know-who. I want more than Jeremy for You to be glorified, but I do also want to love him for my life. Lord, I know that I will love him 'til the day I die, I just pray You'd make a way for us to love a long life. I'm absolutely blessed to be in love with him, and Lord, because I love him, so I ask one more time, help me to deny myself and think of Your will first. Help me to also think of what's best for Jeremy.*

*Lord, You know how it hurts me so remembering the pain I brought him, and You also know I have cried many tears at the thought of hurting him again. So, I pray that when You grant the time for me to share my love, that You'd guard his heart and grant him strength from You. Help him love me without fear if I'm the woman for his life, but help him know Your will before he ever thinks of me for his wife. How I love him, and know I will love him dearly so, how my heart is committed to it all even if he never will let go. I know my love will be strong and faithful to the end of my life, so help him see how true this is and how You've so blessed me. I pray he would continually think of You, and dear Lord, I also pray You would remind him of me, too. Bless him with the desire to come and be with me, so I can share of this great mystery.*

*Jesus, I have faith that a miracle of love could stir in his heart as I pray, and in his family, too. I know as You changed my heart, if Your will was to be so, that You could also change Jeremy and the entire Camp family, too. May they have a heart for You, and as they pray and seek, show them a new light in me that Jeremy will come see. Prepare me for a life with him physically or not, for I'll always lift him up in prayer whether with him or not. I pray only if I could be a blessing and encouragement, only if I could help him fall more in love with You. I only want to bless him with love and happiness. So if my life and love will do that, then I pray and say Amen. Give Jean-Luc and Mike and all his friends wisdom so the counsel he receives wouldn't discourage him from seeing me. I pray Mr. and Mrs. Camp would have a vision from You, Lord, that opens their eyes to see if You have blessed Jeremy with me. Do a miracle in all of us to love You more each day, and only if Your perfect will be, bless us this very day. I will continue to trust in You. My faith rests assured that if Your plan has Jeremy to be my man, You'll work it out for sure. I love You, Lord, and the very fact that You love me blows me away. So I will give You my life now and want everything to be Your way.*

Melissa began praying to meet Jeremy's parents. A year before, when Jeremy had wanted to take her home to Indiana to meet his family, she panicked. She was only nineteen and thought their relationship was going way too fast. Now she had to meet them. So she prayed—and I prayed with her for her heart's desire. And guess what? They came out from Indiana and came over to our house with Jeremy and his brothers to meet her. She was thrilled to meet his family. Before they left, Lis took Jeremy aside and told him she wanted to talk to him and tell him something. As his parents left, Jeremy told them, "Melissa is going to tell me she loves me." Melissa again picked up her journal to write.

Her joy was writing to the Lord, telling Him details of her day and continuing her prayers for Jeremy and those she loved.

*May 14, 2000*

*O Lord, tonight was an amazing night and a beautiful and amazing evening. In fact, I feel I've learned so much and have grown even closer to You this very day. Lord, I see how amazing You are to work through the love of mothers that so bless our lives. I saw how from the prayer to the service to the soul talk afterwards, You were glorified. Jesus, You're so rad. Thank You for my church, The Rock. It's an amazing body of believers, and I'm so blessed. Thank You also for reminding me tonight of the joy and the reward that You bring us. I wait upon You. I pray Your spirit would protect Jeremy and that You would be glorified through his actions. Lord, I also pray as I wait for him to call or come and see me that You would give me the patience and faith to trust in you. Lord, if Tuesday night he's at his house, I thank You and ask You to prepare one talk that we may draw close together through You. But no matter when it is, I know to wait and that it will all work out in its perfect timing. Thank You for family, and for all the blessings they bring. Thank You for my brothers and sisters in the Lord also. You're an almighty God, and I love you. Protect me from any fears, and may I rest in Your arms, falling asleep in the arms of my Jesus. I love You and want for more, and I love Jeremy and attempt to patiently await his love. I can do all things through Christ who strengthens me. Amen. I ♡ U!*

*O, sweet Lord, how Your goodness never ceases. I feel as if I'm the most spoiled Christian woman alive. You're so good to me, and why I'll never know. Lord, thank You, thank You for putting it on my heart to wait upon You. This morning, actually beginning last night, I felt I knew Jeremy was going to come over, and I was right! He came over with his whole family (except April). Well, I didn't see him then, but was sure able to see him today. It's so funny, because my dad had gotten Jeremy's phone number from someone last night, and this morning they were wanting me to call him. But I knew You would give him the strength to take his first step towards me, and that's exactly what happened.*

*Lord, You're so good to me, and Your faithfulness goes beyond anything. You're so amazing, Lord, I'm in awe of You. Jesus, when I saw Jeremy's parents, I felt like they're the love and family I always prayed my husband would have. Lord, they are so wonderful, and they all just shine with You,*

*Jesus. When Mr. Camp prayed for me, I felt the power of Your love coming forth through his voice. O, Lord, how amazing they are. And even more, I see how Jeremy has learned his love for You from his family. Wow! Lord, that's so incredible. And when Jeremy held my hand, he beat me by a second, for I was on my way to grab his. O, Lord, how I love him and am so ready to tell him! You're amazing! Lord, I can hardly believe I'm going to see him tomorrow, and that I'm going to be able to tell him that I've fallen in love with him. Jesus, I see in his eyes that You've prepared him for the most wonderful news of our lives—that the Almighty Lord, who has blessed us with loving us first, has blessed us with the love of each other.*

*Hey Lord, my Love, I love You so much, my dear sweet Father! It's so awesome to realize that when other guys flirt with me, that it's Jeremy that I love. I absolutely love him. I know it's Jeremy my heart beats for and my eyes long to see. Lord, I'm so blessed to have the opportunity to love him now and for all my life. I'm so blessed to share a part in his life in prayer, and Lord willing in matrimony one day. Lord, I pray that You would send angels around him, guarding him everywhere he goes, that he may be used by You all the days of his life. Lord, my soul is so excited that I can hardly even breathe. I'm more honored than anything to be in love with a man like him. Lord, you have done so much in my life, and I feel even now You're continuing to do things.*

*I know Jeremy's love for me will be able to endure all these trials cancer will bring, and that you have the power to bless our lives together. I pray his family would hear You speaking to their hearts about Your good and perfect will for Jeremy, and that they'd support and encourage him to do what his heart desires. Thank You for the love we share and for Your powerful hand that's bringing us together. May I seek Your will no matter what it is, and be patiently awaiting Your will. I do want what's best to glorify You and what's best to make Jeremy happy. So if my love will grant his life joy and happiness, I pray together we will be. But if I bring him sorrow and pain, I pray You'd give him wisdom to see. Lord, You're awesome, and I pray Ryan and Chris would draw closer to You through seeing our lives. I love You, Lord. Amen.*

*Jesus, today is the day I'm going to share my heart with Jeremy. I am so excited, Lord. Today's Tuesday, and I'm anxiously awaiting telling him I love him. I know You say to be anxious for nothing but in prayer and supplication . . . pray always without ceasing. So I'm praying now for today, that this would be a beautiful day and that You'd be glorified throughout all I say. I pray for my dear, sweet Jeremy. I know he must be going through a hard time with all of this, but I ask You to give him faith as big as a mustard seed and hope in Your faithfulness. I pray if he does love me, that You would bring us together today without any fear. I pray he wouldn't be afraid to love me, but willing, if that's what would make him the most happy. Sweet Jesus, I look at him and see into his soul and love every bit I see. I look at his parents and brothers and see complete unconditional love that comes from You, Jesus.*

*You're so amazing to allow me to even know the Camp family. How I can't wait to meet April and her husband and Meka! Lord, this is a joy like no other. Of course, it in no way compares to the depth and width of Your love, but it's amazing in itself. O, Jesus, I pray for a miracle today. I pray that Jeremy and I would be able to spend time alone, and that I wouldn't feel sick during that time. O Lord, I see You doing something more incredible than words can describe. I see You using this cancer to bring Jeremy and I together. I can't even hardly wait for him to know that I love him! This is so exciting. I pray You would prepare his heart before he comes over and give him the same peace and joy that You've given me. Lord, I pray for his father and mother, Mr. and Mrs. Camp, that they would be encouraged and uplifted at this pastors' conference. I pray for Jeremy's younger brothers, that they would have a wonderful, fun time here in California and most of all here with sweet Jeremy. I pray they would look up to him and their father and desire to be like them. I pray for April and her husband and child, that they would be very close to You, Lord, and that You'd pour out blessings on them. I thank You for the dear Camp family. I thank You that they have Your precious love pouring out of them, and that it's beautiful! I thank You for brothers and sisters like them. They are amazing, God, and You alone are awesome.*

*Lord, as I listen to The Kry, I realize I need to thank You for them. Thank You for Jean-Luc and how he has blessed Jeremy's life with friendship, good counsel, and help into music ministry. Lord, You're amazing. Thank You for the powerful messages that pour through their songs. I pray You would continue to use them abundantly to bless Christians and to go deeper in their commitment to You and use them to open the lost unto salvation! Amen.*

*I pray for my family, beginning with those I hardly know in Canada and New Mexico and anywhere else. Thank You for the generations of* believers. I pray that if there are any non-Christians, You'd save them. I lift up my Grandma and Grandpa Henning. I pray they would continue to see You work through this and Your name would be glorified. I pray Grandma Vivian would be strong and not afraid, full of love and peace to enjoy her life with You 'til the end. I pray for my dear parents. I ask that Your strength would continue to flow into them. I pray that Dad would fall more in love with You by seeing and enduring this trial of cancer. I pray Mom would realize continually that my life is not my own, and it is only by Your amazing grace I've been given twenty years, and by your grace and mercy I'll be given more. Lord, may Heather not fear and worry about my health one bit. I pray she'd diligently finish school and safely return home. I know You'll bless her life with continually knowing You more and more.

Dear gracious and loving God, what amazing grace You give. I love You so dearly to save a wretch like me. I was once lost, and by Your grace I'm found. I was so blind, and now I'll forever thank You for giving me eyes to see! Lord, I see Ryan and see an amazing man. I see dedication, commitment, hard work, and most of all love. I see love pouring out of him and desiring to do so all the time. So I pray the fear and hard trials that come in between him surrendering over all his love would cease. Give him Your strength to be a lover of God. I thank You for how he blesses me. He is such a wonderful brother; I ask he'd just surrender it all to You. I do pray for his heart for Melissa, what a doll, but I ask they'd both be 100 percent in love with You first! I know Your love is all that we need, and all that they need to be happy. As You will, bring them closer together in Your timing. Lord, You're so awesome.

I thank You also for my little sister, Meggie, what a woman she's grown up to be, but a little sister she will forever be to me. Thank You for her joy no matter what rocks come her way. Thank You for her laugh I'm blessed to hear each day. Thank You for her smile that brightens my eyes to shine and thank You for her friendship that's brought me through many a hardship. Thank You for her beauty that shines from within and out, and most of all I thank You, Lord, for her love for You. May she grow to be a woman devoted to You, and may Your grace and kindness patiently see her through. Thank You for her prom and the beautiful dress she wears. Thank You for Tyler and all the fun they share. Please continue to bless her high school years and always wipe away her every fear and tears. I ♡ U! King of my life, Sovereign God above.

*So, it's with this I end my prayer and send my unfailing love. Not because I am strong for You, no, I'm very weak, but it's by Your might I'll forever fight this spiritual battle I'm in. So, know I ♡ love you more today than even I have before, and with my love I give my life, please take it, my dear Lord. For when You reign in my flesh, I'm more happy than can be, for You're the lover of my soul, my joy, my everything. I'm willing to be healthy with joy—that sounds so great—but if health isn't Your perfect plan, I'm willing once again.*

*Use me, however You desire, whichever way You may, and all I ask is for the faith to trust You all the way. Whether with my head full of hair or bald from head to toe, there is one thing I'll always say and forever will let be known: You are my Lord, and I remain in Your mighty hand, so it's by Your grace and might alone I am able even to stand. So, if beauty or homeliness is what my face will be, I will continue to let my dear Christ shine and always reign in me.*

*Our God reigns—may I proclaim it to Zion.*

*Lord, I'm going to sleep and trust You with every moment I live. And forever I will thank You for this joy You so graciously give. You are so loving and so great, thank You once again, and now it's in Your hands I lay myself once again. Hallelujah, praise the Lord! Amen!*

The next day Jeremy called, and they talked on the phone as he was driving his brothers to the zoo. It was a nice conversation, and then they said goodbye. Melissa was bummed. "Mom, why didn't I just ask him if I could go with him?" I called out upstairs to her, "Go with him!"

"OK, I'm calling him back!"

"Mom, he said he was almost at the zoo, but he turned around and he's coming to get me!" She was so excited!

It was a beautiful day, and Melissa loved every minute—Melissa, Jeremy, and his brothers, Jared and Josh, at the zoo.

That night Mark and I entertained Jeremy's brothers downstairs while Lis and Jeremy went upstairs to her room. This was her opportunity. I could see the excitement and joy on her face. She had no idea of Jeremy's prayer to God, "If you want me to marry her, she has to tell me she loves me." She just had this compelling need to tell him she loved him, so she did! That night Melissa told Jeremy, "I love you." He told her that if he were to tell her he loved her, too, that would mean marriage. All or nothing with Jeremy; if you love each other, you get married!

*Lord Jesus, thank You for giving me yesterday. Tuesday (5-16) was the day I told Jeremy I love him. What a privilege and an honor to tell him that! I'm so excited to write everything to You. First, last night I couldn't sleep a wink. I was like a little kid who knew Disneyland awaited me tomorrow, but it was even better. Instead, I was a woman who awaited telling the man of my dreams that I love him. Oh, what a privilege and delight to love You, Christ my Lord, and Jeremy! So, as You know, I woke up at 6:00 a.m. or so and had to force myself to sleep. I didn't want to have bags under my eyes, but I also wanted to be ready at any moment to see him as soon as he would call. Finally I woke up at 8:00 a.m. and had my breakfast with Mom and then got ready. I was so excited all day, every moment, even while waiting.*

*Lord, I felt as I was getting ready that You were preparing the day. How special of You to do so. So, when Lindsey came over and nearly blew my ears off that I'd get to see him, that was funny. Finally, while I was on the phone to Emma, he called. But he was going to take Joshua and Jared to the zoo first and then come see me around 5:30 or 6:00. That was exciting, but also devastating, thinking I'd have to wait that long to see him. So, my mom yelled up from downstairs, "Go with him," and Emma told me to call him back, so I did! Lord, what extreme boldness You've given me for him. I love it! So, when I called it was cute. (I hope he really did want me to go!) I asked if he wanted alone time with his brothers, and he asked if I wanted to go. Of course, I told him, "Yes!" And I asked him to ask his brothers if they minded, and before I knew it, they were on their way to get me.*

*What an extreme blessing to be able to spend the day with Jeremy and his two brothers. First, I have to tell you, Lord, they are amazing. Joshua is just a cutie in a half. He has such a great character and laugh and love for You. In fact, they all do. And when Josh held my hand—I could have melted. That meant so much to me! And then there's Jared, what a cool guy! It blew me away how much he loves you, Lord; you can just see it. He is so fun and polite and a great brother! Lord, I admire how he looks after Josh and enjoys being his bud and also how he adores Jeremy.*

*Now, looking back, I feel bad, as if I should have let them be alone and enjoy each other's company. Thank You for having Jared be such a cool guy that he treated me so well and nicely. I was so blessed to get to know them. Lord, I pray they would continue to grow closer to You and more in love with You. Also, protect cute Jared from bad girls! That's so cute how he gave the wrong number to those girls who were flirting with him. I pray the time they all have left together would be blessed and multiplied. As much as I want to see Jeremy, I thank You for his love for his family and putting them first. It's how it should be, Lord.*

*I admired watching Jeremy and Jared taking care of Josh when he slipped and hurt himself. Of course, I wish that I was the one to fall, poor Josh, but I think he handled it well. O, Lord, You knew that when Jeremy prayed, because of my great love for You, I melted. The love my heart holds for You and him is amazing! I loved the tram ride and when the little girl talked to me and Jeremy looked for every opportunity to witness. So rad! Lord, You are my love, and it's awesome seeing that love in Jeremy. May it always and forever shine bright for You!*

*I thank You for everything, the entire day. For Jeremy giving me my ticket to buying me a water. He's just so thoughtful and sweet! All of the Camps are, what a blessing. I do pray for them. I thank You for allowing me to even know such a dear family, let alone love them. I pray spiritual blessings and protection, and that You would do a mighty and awesome work in their lives continually! Lord, I want to finish telling You what happened. I know You know, but You're my best friend, and I want You to know sharing this with You is just as important—and more—than sharing it with anyone else! So, Lord, we finally left, and by this time I'm thinking I love this man and I want this man to be my husband and the father of our children! Big stuff!*

*Lord, the other day I didn't get to finish telling You about my time with Jeremy, Jared, and Joshua (Tuesday, May 16). I had such a wonderful time talking with Jared and holding Josh's hand. I absolutely adored seeing how Jared so loves Jeremy, and Jeremy loves Jared. What a beautiful picture of family. I pray for them. I was selfish and wanting to be with Jeremy and should have let them all be alone together. So, Lord, I pray the fast moments they have together today would be amazing! I think of sitting on the tram and Jared and Josh should have had spots by Jeremy. Sorry for not thinking of that! I pray Jared didn't get his feeling hurt I didn't think of it. So, Lord, on the tram while I was freezing to death, I put my arm under Jeremy's. How I wished he knew I loved him then, but I still had to wait to share. So, the day was amazing, and everything was so special. Thank You, Lord, for allowing me to go and feel so well. That was a great blessing.*

*Lord, then we left and were at In-N-Out Burger, and I let him know I didn't want to take away from his brothers but would still like to talk to him if I could. So, at home after he told my parents and I about the "pastors and their daughters" who want to marry him, I finally was able to take him upstairs. Again, Jared and Josh were so sweet and "go with the flow"; they're great!*

*So, finally the part where I told him my love revelation. We sat down on the bed and got all cozy, and then I realized how nervous I was. So, by Your wisdom, we prayed, and then my fear was gone. This was the biggest thing I ever was going to say. I began by telling him how I've been praying for him for a long time, and his family and everything. His face was so cute, I could tell he was thinking, "Spit it out, Melissa!" So I told him You had put it on my heart to pray and fast for him and me, and I did. I told him how I was praying and asking the Lord if I loved him. Yes, that's what I was praying. And I told him, "I do. I love you, Jeremy! I know, I know." Then I was mumbling something, and I think that's when he came in and kissed me. How I love and long to kiss him. I just know when the timing is right, we will make such an on-fire couple, that love You first and always, and then one another.*

*I know he loves me, but he's just scared. In fact, he said he was, and we cried. And I told him how before I knew I had cancer (thinking there was like a one percent chance), I had asked You to heal me for him, and I know You have and that this chemotherapy will kill all the microscopic cancer cells left. I will not be afraid, but only believe (Mark 5:36).*

*But at the same time, I know Your ways*
*and thoughts are not mine, and You*
*may choose to do a work I never*
*thought You'd do. And if You*
*do, that's OK, because Your plan*
*is that good, perfect,*
*and pleasing will of God!*

So, Jesus, I told him I love him and will all my life but want him to have happiness and blessings. And I know if I am the woman that will bring him happiness, blessings, and most importantly closer to You, I know You'll bring us together! I trust You, Lord, and rely only on Your love. I know Jeremy has love for me, too, but he has a spirit of fear. You say in Your Word that perfect love casts our fear, so if his heart holds a perfect love for me, please in Your power cast out his fear!

*You're so mighty to heal and to save, to give*
*strength to the weak, health to the sick, love*
*to the lonely, truth through Your Word, sight*
*to the blind, wealth to the poor, peace to the*
*loner, and faith to Your children.*

Lord, I have peace to love Jeremy for my whole life. I have the hope to know I'm in Your hands and my life belongs to You. So, my precious Jesus, I know You're watching over me and my precious Jeremy, and whatever Your perfect will may be, You know it is well with me. Speak to Jeremy during this time; may he know if he is to be mine. Give him love, peace, joy, and happiness to know Your will for him. And continue to give me every day Your strength and patience to sit at Your feet and wait for You to speak.

*Telling him I love him now and always will was the most beautiful thing I've ever said. I felt as he kissed me and held me close that You were smiling, too! Lord, being with him makes me feel pure and even closer to you. I do believe with all my heart that Jeremy is the man for me, so no matter what he's going through, I'll wait until eternity. However long this time will be, I have the faith to endure, for my love for him I can't erase, and it is worth any amount of time. I'd rather live all my life knowing I waited for him, than ever even thinking of compromising. It's amazing how powerful true love can be. So, with that power I will wait for You to work in Jeremy! You have my word and hold my heart, as You do his, and we both know we can no longer fight what our hearts already know. As I lay in his arms and felt his body close with mine, I know it's love that holds me there and will for all my life. Please grant him the strength to let go of any and every fear so he can know how much I long to tell and share my love with him. I cast all my cares for Jeremy down at Your feet and know You'll work something out in Your perfect timing. As we were talking Tuesday night, he asked me where I see myself. And I responded I didn't want to scare him, but I see myself with him. I know the Lord has done a work, a complete 180 degrees in me, and I even know going to Calvary Chapel Bible College is completely dependent on Jeremy.*

*He held me and kissed me again and again (as I wished it would never end), then I told him how I'd even move to Indiana, which I even have a desire to do. I feel it's there we may live, and he'll be most happy. And Jesus, You know that's all I want—to love You and Jeremy! When he asked me if I was going to freak out in two weeks and say, "I can't love two men," I thought how privileged I am to love You and him. He's so funny and cute and hot and all I will ever want! I even told him how I don't deserve him, and he said he doesn't deserve me. I told him how I love kissing him and want to all my life, him and only him. And I think he feels the same way. I could tell he wanted to tell me that he loves me, too, but I felt You tell me to say wait and pray to see what to do. I know that gave him comfort, to know he need not say anything but can just enjoy knowing I'm in love with him.*

*I pray, Lord Jesus, that he understands I'm committed to loving him, and that it's not because I'm sick but because I've been seeking You. I pray he understands it's love I'd love to receive from him, but if that's just too hard, it's OK. I pray he would feel no pressure, not thinking twice of my situation but completely seek Your face and ask for spiritual wisdom. I know in my heart we will have a long and wonderful life together. But I also know he may not want the trials I'm now faced with. So, once again, I pray the same prayer I prayed with him, that my dear Lord will show him what's holding him back. If it's fear that keeps him from enjoying the love I long to give, then dear Lord, take that away and give him peace and joy! But then again, if it's You that's holding him from my love, then may he know without a doubt You have another plan in store.*

*I have in the past and will continue to trust, wait, and hope only, solely in You. I know Jeremy is a man and a sinner just like me, and maybe he will fight Your will just like the old me. If he does, I pray You would graciously show him how to trust in You with everything, even the love he has for me. I'm sure he's deeply afraid of many things, and rightfully so. But, Jesus, there is one thing I will forever and always know: this life I live, and Jeremy's, too, belongs not to ourselves but to You, to will and act and do. It's with those promises I read and regain faith again, knowing You will have Your way in my life once again.*

*I do desire that Jeremy would diligently seek Your face, and only by Your almighty power give his heart the grace to love me now, in this condition I am in, knowing You will heal and be glorified once again. For I will testify each day of the power You've worked in me, and how I'd love for him to share that precious gift with me! Wow, Lord, I do trust in You so very much, and it's so beautiful and wonderful, and I love You so very much! I trust my heart with You and him, and will wait to see what You do. Teach me how to be a woman who is completely content with You, so that no matter where I go, I'll always be in love with You. Your love is more than enough to see me through my life, and it's only an abundant blessing to even feel this love for Jeremy. So, whether a life alone with You, or shared with the love of my life, I will be more than content and never think twice. Your will for me is way better than any plan of mine, so it's in Your hands I remain and grow in hope and love.*

"My love for Jeremy will suffer long
and be kind; my love will not envy,
it will not parade itself, I will not
be puffed up; my love will not
behave rudely, will not seek my own will,
not be provoked, will not think evil;
my love will not rejoice in the iniquity
of others, but rejoice in truth, my love
bears all things and believes
all things, hopes all things,
and endures all things.
My love for Jeremy will never fail
(1 Corinthians 13:4-8, paraphrased)."

*Lord, however long, by Your strength I'll wait and pray this prayer, for I know no man in the world, to my eyes, could even compare to him. Amen.*

*Jesus, when Jeremy said, "You know if I tell you I love you, I'm going to ask you to marry me," I said, "I know, and I do." I know by faith I'll be healed, and we will be one through You. So, I will wait upon You, Lord, in awe of all You do. You are so awesome and wonderful and gracious and kind. I praise You, my awesome King, for my life is Yours, please reign. Our God reigns. My God reigns. How beautiful on any land are the feet of those who bring good news, who proclaim peace. I will proclaim peace and good news from Your Word. Strengthen Jeremy to minister and serve You, no matter what the condition of his heart. I pray his parents would have wisdom to help him know Your will, and Jean-Luc, Mike, Damion, Danny, Phil, Jason, Aaron, Charlie—everyone will have wisdom to know what Your will is. You're such a good and loving God. Pour out Your wisdom and grace, and most of all, be glorified! Amen.*

Jeremy left that night telling Melissa that they would talk when he got back from his missions' trip to Colorado in about a week.

# CHAPTER

## 7

# WAITING

*I* was amazed at my daughter's fast recovery and of all the joy she had. I kept thinking how great God was in bringing Jeremy back into her life and letting her experience this romance in the midst of a cancer diagnosis.

*James 5:16: "Confess your trespasses to one another, and pray for one another, that you may be healed. The effective, fervent prayer of a righteous man avails much."*

> Melissa, count it all joy while going through this trial, knowing the testing of your faith produces patience. And let it have its perfect work, so you'll be perfect (mature) and complete, lacking nothing.

*Heavenly Father, I praise Your holy name and thank You for the privilege I have to share my testimony at L.C.C. What an honor, Lord. I ask for wisdom in what to share and what not. I pray this would be all You and none of me. You are so awesome and holy, and I'm so thankful for this privilege. Use me in these kids' lives, and help me be sensitive to know whether or not there are some kids who aren't saved. I thank You in advance for the help You will send me now and as I speak. Prepare their hearts and my lips. Thank You for giving me this gift. Be glorified through my life. Amen.*

Melissa was immediately given the opportunity to give her testimony at her high school, La Costa Canyon. She felt honored and privileged to have the opportunity to speak and considered her cancer a gift—a gift to be used to tell people about her Savior. Her desire was to glorify God through her life and to be used in kids' lives. She was actively seeking out the "one" whose life would be changed. God is so faithful: He answered her prayer overwhelmingly and continues to glorify Himself through her life to this day and to use her in kids' lives. All God's ways are good and kind! He has, does, and will continue to do amazing things through Melissa's life and any life that is completely surrendered to Him.

While Jeremy was in Colorado, Melissa was focused on ministering to others. She wasn't concerned that he didn't tell her he loved her back; she was content to wait on God's timing. She had no idea Jeremy was having a hard time. Jeremy's mother, Teri, called me while he was in Colorado. She asked if Melissa had seen him, and did we know where he was. She was concerned for him because they hadn't heard from him, and they knew he was troubled.

*O Lord, today, a little after I was reading Your Word, Jeremy called. How I want to tell him I love him every moment! He told me that his parents told the pastor whose daughter also likes Jeremy that I'm in love with their son. Which I am! Yes, I am! And Jeremy said that the pastor said, "We still love him, even if he doesn't marry our daughter." First of all, I had no idea Jeremy felt the pressure that if he didn't marry that girl, that the church wouldn't love him. I had no idea. I pray for that situation and ask You, Lord, to be with that pastor and his daughter. I pray they would grow from this, and any hurt feelings would be quickly mended by You. Jeremy also said his parents told him they'll support him whatever he decides, and that they were a shoulder to cry on.*

*How I long to see joy and peace in Jeremy's face and heart! I pray that while he's away in Colorado, You would bless him with an abundant amount of time with You. I know, just as You revealed wisdom to me during my time alone with You, You'll reveal wisdom to Jeremy as he seeks You alone. Lord, I pray he would have wisdom to listen to wise counsel, and discernment to weed out doubts from others. I pray, most of all, that Jeremy will hear Your voice speak to his heart, and that he would know, because of You, if it is me he loves. It's a wonderful and amazing gift to trust my heart to You, Lord. It's so awesome and comforting to know whatever happens, You will work things out.*

> I know Jeremy, and I love You more than any other, and we both desire Your perfect will for our lives to be accomplished. So, precious Lord, I know You will be glorified through my life and Jeremy's, and it's with that hope and joy I trust You with everything.

*I'm not afraid of anything, not even all Jeremy's fear for my heart. I know one day we'll be together. (Heather's here and I'll finish prayer later. I ♡ U Lord)*

## May 19, 2000

*Hey Lord, my dear sweet Jesus and friend, how's it goin'? Funny question, Lord. I just want to begin my day thanking You. Thank You for being Lord of my life and the lover of my soul. I have such joy in loving You. Thank You also for the joy I have in loving Jeremy, too! Lord, it is such a gift to love him the way I do. I finally feel the way I believe he did. My love for him is unconditional. Lord, even if it's too hard for him to see me through chemotherapy, my love for him will remain. I love him so dearly that I just don't want him to go through any pain. Jesus, would you pray for him, a prayer I might not say, to help him through this time apart during his week away? I know You hear his every thought, joy and sadness, too, so I pray Your grace, peace, and joy will patiently see him through.*

*Lord, thinking about him makes me smile and long to hold his hand, so give me the peace no matter what to always understand. Even though I love him now, yesterday, and months ago, I will wait however long it takes for You to let him know. I pray I may comfort him even as I'm far away. I pray my prayer will give him strength to lean on You today. Jesus, remember how You've used Jeremy to bring me close to You? Now, dear Lord, You know that that's all I want to do. I pray my life, friendship, and love will encourage him to take a deeper step towards falling in love with You, Lord. It's so amazing how You use him every moment in my life, and now if it's Your will, someday I wish to be his wife. It's funny how in the past I would always hate being called "girlfriend." I remember in high school, being introduced as a girlfriend, and thinking, "I don't belong to you." Now I find my heart in a condition too foreign, because I realize I can't wait to tell everyone I love Jeremy! When he asked if I'd mind if he told others of my love, I thought, please do, I can't wait for everyone to know! I know I love him very much, and will for all my life, so Jesus my first love and King, do a mighty work in me.*

*I pray all our lives, beginning now, we will turn to You before each other and always know that it is You who gave us the gift of each other. Jesus, I feel I know in faith that I am healed of cancer. And also, I feel in faith Jeremy and I will be together. I pray if my vision is clouded by the intent of my heart, that You, dear Lord, would prepare me for whatever is to* come. You're awesome, and You know the best medicine in my life, my King and Master and Lord of lords, giver of peace and all things. I trust You, my faithful Lord. I know You're my awesome God who delights in doing miracles and bringing two people together to be one. Give us a joy to be together (I already have that!). As Jeremy's in Colorado, I see You doing things in his life without me, and that brings me joy. For even though I want to marry him NOW, I know You still have a plan to work through us a ministry he can do single and one I can do single. So use us apart until You use us together. I love You, Lord, and I love Jeremy. Pour out Your love, strength, joy, and happiness into his heart today. Give him Your power to minster and serve others with joy. Remind him that I love him unconditionally.

*Saturday, May 20, 2000*

Dear Lord,

Today was a hard day. But You know the moment I got on my knees; Your help was poured out. Jesus, what I realized today was that this cancer I have is a BIG deal. I know You've seen in my heart the faith and belief that I'm healed, and that chemotherapy will heal me free from any recurrence of this cancer. But Lord, I never thought I may be wrong. I didn't really think the cancer recurring could even be an option. Lord, I believe I've always been willing for whatever Your will is, it's just that I've believed Your will is to heal me, bring me closer to You, and bless Jeremy and me with the gift of each other. So today, when faced with the reality that Jeremy may not choose to walk through this valley—it hit hard when my mom and I were praying tonight and she said, "even though this is a path Jeremy would have never chosen to go through." Lord, I hadn't put myself in his shoes completely until then. Now all I want to do is talk to him and ask him how he's doing. I want to know how he's handling all of this, what he needs and how I can help. My heart longs to comfort his and be there for him.

Dear Lord, I do pray for Jeremy's emotions, spiritual welfare, and physical being. I know You can hear all his heart's emotions and protect him from pain. It's also stunned me how when I was sharing with one of my parents how I don't want him to hurt, they said the only thing that would do that is health. So, now my prayer is changing from protection of pain to a deeper relationship, faith, commitment, longing, desire, and love for You through this time. I know with all my heart, as my mom *shared, Your timing is perfect, and even though many will say this is bad timing, it is Your timing. My sweet Jesus, how I love You and ask You to take that banner of love that's over Jeremy and wrap him in it and bring him comfort. My mom was saying how...*

> *... trials like these are what make a great man of God, and I believe it!*

*Even though I would never choose Jeremy to walk this road with me, even though there are times like today that I wish I didn't love him solely for the reason he wouldn't be hurt knowing of all I have to continue to go through so he wouldn't even have the possibility of going through this with me.*

*But Lord, I love him so much, and I can't fight it—there's no way. And my heart feels he is feeling the same way. I'm sure he wishes he didn't love me so he wouldn't have to go through this, but there's definitely no denying it. Jeremy and I are in love. Lord, as we were talking in my room last Tuesday night and laughing and crying and hugging and kissing, I realized there is no other man I ever want to be with than him. I've known this for a while now, and it just continues to grow deeper and stronger each day.*

*Dear Lord, thank You that my heart is in Your hands, and even though my heart has grown so deep and wide for the love of Jeremy inside, I pray You'd grant me peace and faith to trust in You. Lord, I pray You'd bless Jeremy with mighty men of You that will counsel him to walk in Your ways and praise You through this. I pray his heart and mind would not get discouraged, but we would lift up our voices to the sky and tell everyone that our God reigns. Lord, I pray You'd put it on Jeremy's heart when to call me and what to say. Put it on his heart through time alone with You whether or not to commit to loving me. I pray Wednesday he'd fly home safely and be strengthened to play for Mike's new church. I also* pray You'd bless the time we get to be together, whether Wednesday night or Thursday. I'm longing for the time. Lord, I pray You'd prepare me for that time to encourage Jeremy and love him unconditionally. I want to love him even if he turns his back on me. He needs our love, Lord. I know he'll eternally enjoy Yours. I only pray for the privilege to enjoy my love for a lifetime. Lord, would You bless these next few days, weeks, months, and year to be an awesome time of drawing nearer to You and one another? I love You, Lord, and pray the prayer Jeremy always prayed for me: I pray I may fall more in love with You! I also pray Jeremy would fall more in love with You and lean on You alone. I ♡ U – Amen

*May 21, 2000*

Dear Sweet Jesus,

How I love You so! Jesus, my heart is so satisfied when it's in You I rest. Thank You for giving me my family and friends that have continually supported me to look to You. Jesus, You are so amazing and wonderful, and I am more than privileged to live my life for You. I do pray that today I would think of how to glorify You first and always. I pray for the strength to deny my flesh and pick up my cross and follow You. Thank You for paying the high price for my sins so I may live a pure, clean, spotless life as unto You. Jesus, You're so amazing, and I love You so much! Jesus, I also can't believe the verse my eyes fell upon today, what comfort it brought me to read Acts 27:34. "Therefore I urge you to take nourishment, for this is for your survival, since not a hair will fall from the head of any of you." Jesus, I would love for my hair to remain in, and as soon as the chemo is over, to marry my love Jeremy. But I will be faithful to nourish my body and take care as much as possible, and then allow You to do the rest. Lord, I'm all for You healing my bod and keeping in my hair—miracles are greatly welcomed, so my sweet Jesus, have Your way in me and be now glorified. I love You; I do! I'll give You my life and all that I am. Love You! Praise You, I worship Your mighty name, now and forever! Amen.

Lord, I pray for wisdom and what to pray! I'm scared and sad and upset, and the only person I want to see is the only person I can't. Jesus, I want to see or even hear Jeremy's voice. I miss him and need him so! I don't want him to have to go through this, but I don't think I can go through it alone. I need You, Jesus, because my heart wants Jeremy, and I want to be near him and have him near me. But I can't get upset if he doesn't call or visit. I need to trust in You!

*Lord, I cast all my cares and fears at Your feet,
and I ask for Your strength to fill me. Prepare me
to walk and fight this valley ahead of me.*

*Prepare Jeremy and my family and friends. I love You, Lord, and thank You that You will bring us through this. Forgive me for getting upset and snappy tonight, it's because everyone I see isn't Jeremy, and I need his hugs right now. So, pour out Your love on me and on Jeremy. Maybe he's hurting for me and himself. Please comfort him with the same comfort You give me. I love You. Help me sleep and even dream about You or the future blessings Your Word will bestow! I love You, Lord! Help me lean on You for strength and help me be peaceful and joyful with Your light shining through. Help me deny my flesh so You may be glorified. I pray You'd allow this medicine to heal my body of any cancer ever again, and I pray Your hands could miraculously hold my hair in my head. O, how I love You, Jesus! Praise Your mighty works You'll continue to do. Amen.*

We met with Dr. Koonings, Melissa's oncologist. He told us that he had the original tumor reevaluated by a pathologist and just got the news. Remember how they told us it was "just an ovarian cyst"? No, it wasn't—it was cancer. The first pathologist was wrong; it was not benign, it was malignant. Melissa's surgeon was wrong, the radiologist was wrong, and the pathologist was wrong! They had all made mistakes. Melissa had ovarian cancer, but it was a different kind than we normally hear of. It was a granulosa cell tumor. The correct treatment in the beginning should have been to open up her abdomen and remove the entire tumor, leaving it intact. Exactly like the "scary" doctor had told Melissa when he said, "You sure went to the wrong doctor." Dr. Koonings said this type of cancer is encapsulated, and if it had been removed properly, she wouldn't have needed any other treatment—no chemo—no life threat! The original surgeon, who was so proud of his laparoscopic prowess, had dissected the tumor inside of her, causing the cancer to spread throughout her body. Dr. Koonings' nurse, Cathy, told me that when he went over her records, he put his head down on his desk and wept.

He then gave us a chemotherapy doctor that he said he would use for his own children. He seemed to really care for Melissa, and we trusted him. She had to wait about three weeks for her surgery to heal, and then chemo would begin. This was devastating news. All of us had prayed for the right doctor—the best doctor. I remembered the staff offering us another surgeon because he was late. I remembered saying, "No we are waiting for the best doctor." Amid my mind running through all the mistakes and bad decisions, the Lord reminded me that HE is in control, then and now. There are no mistakes that He does not oversee for His purposes. This was His plan, and we knew He had something amazing for our daughter. She was His, and we knew it!

We met with the medical oncologist, the doctor that decides and oversees chemotherapy. He gave us great hope and told us that this cancer had an 80 percent cure rate. We were encouraged.

The first day of chemotherapy was harder on me than Melissa. We walked into the chemo room and saw lots of those Barcalounger recliner chairs, IV drips, and people much older than Melissa. It was a large room, with about twenty big chairs, all Pepto-Bismol pink. It looked a little bit like a pedicure shop, except there wasn't any tubs of hot water to relax your feet, no massage rollers to release the tension in your back, and no one pampering and massaging your feet or adding any color to your toes. There wasn't any music playing or lights to brighten the room. I said to the nurse, "This should be me, not my daughter."

"No, Mom! Don't say that. It should not be you," Melissa said with intensity and correction in her voice. She chose a lounge chair to sit in. The nurse put in IVs and attached the chemo bags. The drip, drip began. No one prepared Melissa for what to expect. We had no idea except for the stories we saw in movies. I expected the worst and would not leave her side. After about thirty minutes, Melissa was visibly uncomfortable and in distress but not voicing what was wrong. She didn't want to make a fuss. At my insistence, she told me she was itching all over—an obvious allergic reaction. I rushed to get the nurse. She said that some patients have this kind of reaction and called the doctor. He prescribed some Benadryl to relieve the itch. It finally worked, but it was an intense first introduction to chemotherapy.

We were in that darkened, unseemly room for about four hours. We didn't talk much. We both read our Bibles, journaled, and prayed silently. It was a habit of mine to read through the Bible or read through a book in the Bible and write down what the Lord was teaching me through it. But today I just wanted God to lead me to a verse or passage that I needed right at this moment. I asked the Lord to reveal a Scripture that He wanted to speak to me through. This became a habit through the journey of chemotherapy and hospital visits. We began to write down Scriptures on note cards of the promises God would reveal to us in His Word.

That first appointment, I was led to Psalm 21. That day I wrote above it: "Jeremy's & Melissa's 5/22/00"

It is titled "Joy in the Salvation of the Lord"

I began to pray this Psalm for them every day throughout our journey:

*Amen! Thank You, Lord, for giving Mom and I this promise in Your holy Word. Amen!*

*I shall have joy in Your strength, O L<small>ORD</small>;
And in Your salvation how greatly shall
I rejoice! You have given me my heart's
desire, and have not withheld the request of
my lips. For You meet me with the blessings
of goodness; You set a crown of pure gold
upon my head. I asked life from You, and
You gave it to me—Length of days forever
and ever.*

P<small>SALM</small> *21:1-4*

I know God answered this prayer and blessed both of them with this promise—not the way I thought He would, but in a way that far surpassed my ability to comprehend at that moment.

> *Jesus, today's Monday, May 22, my first day of chemotherapy, and I praise You, Lord! You are so mighty and worthy to be praised. I pray that Jeremy's heart would praise You, Lord. I pray he would know if it's health You're giving me. Jesus, I'm sorry for having a selfish attitude lately, I was so wrong! And as Miles said, I need to ask You one thing I need to change. Change my heart's attitude towards myself and others. Lord, I pray I may look to my family and friends and think before I speak. I want to be closer to You, and through that, love my brothers and sisters in Christ and everyone with the love that comes from You. Thank You for Pam, my Christian sister who was able to encourage me so. May I pray for them all. May I pray for the women and men going through cancer. May You*

*use me to help fight this disease and bring others to be drawn into You. Jesus, Your plan each day amazes me. I realize how I am such an awful sinner, and yet by running to You, we're together. I want to laugh and cry and be with You. I want to be closer to You through this process than ever. I thank You for the chemotherapy that's in my body now and how it is killing the bad cells.*

*Jesus, I praise You—no matter what.*

*Help me when it's hard, help me when pain comes, or even when hair goes. You're my help, and I trust You! Lord, I'm choosing to be a woman of grace and prayer.*

*I would love if You could change me from a selfish person to a selfless person, and I would look to the needs of others rather than my needs. I pray, Jesus, for wisdom in how to treat my friends and family and feel Your freedom to be led by You. I pray for Mom, Dad, and Grandma, Grandpa and Grandma, Ryan, Heather, Meggie, Ashley, Lindsey, Emma, Sarah, Natalie, Jessica, all the Christians (brothers and sisters), and Jeremy Camp.*

*I pray, Lord Jesus, You'd give them Your eyes to see and Your faith to know I'm in Your hands and You have and will turn what was bad into what will glorify You!*

*Lord, I pray for Jeremy today as he's in Colorado. You know how I wish he were waiting at home when I come, but even though we can't be together physically, I ask You, Holy Spirit, to pray for him and me as if we were. I know his love for me aches for my pain, as my love for him aches that he sees and knows of the pain my body has, Lord. Take our hearts and bind them to be a strong tower. I pray our relationship would be based on You always, in our actions, heart, mind, thoughts, in everything. I pray our tower will be built on faith and the solid chief cornerstone of You, our Lord Jesus Christ. I pray as my soul tastes the water You give to me, Jeremy's life would have that, too. Lord, I want Jeremy to lean back on Your chest as You hold him and tell him things will be OK.*

*You know, Lord, I am so blessed that You blinded my eyes from seeing Jeremy is the man I've always prayed for. I'm so grateful You waited to reveal that to me through prayer, fasting, and waiting upon You. Now I think and pray for him every day, all day, without ever ceasing. He is so a part of me, even when my flesh cries out, "NO! He doesn't deserve this!" I know there's nothing—even cancer, surgery, chemotherapy, and baldness—nothing will come between the love You've placed in my heart and Jeremy's heart for each other. I want to say to him, "Jeremy, just let me love you. All I ever wanted to do was love you back, now I ask you to just let me love you."*

*Lord, I pray Jeremy is seeking You on his face, before the Lord, and that You and I will intercede for him during this hard time. Jesus, open my eyes and heart to see the Scriptures dear sweet Jeremy needs. Open my ears to listen to him and understand what he's going through. Jesus, I want to continue to pray for him without ceasing, knowing that his life is in Your hands, as is mine, and*

*Your power will protect us to bring glory to Your holy Name. You know Jeremy and I commit our lives to loving, serving, honoring, worshiping, repenting, glorifying, and magnifying You, Jesus.*

*God, You are good, and I pray now a verse You gave my mom and I, and I pray in faith Your Word would be magnified truthfully through our willing life. I love You, Jesus Christ, my Lord, Savior, my God, my Alpha and my Omega. May You be praised. Jeremy's heart and mine are in the hand of the Lord, like the river of water He turns wherever He wishes.*

*Lord, You know You have my heart, and I will continually seek yours. Jesus, I want You to take my life and lead me wherever You will. All I want to do is meditate upon You, but at times it seems just too hard. Oh, precious Lord and God above, I'm blessed to love You, but I pray to You this night that You'd be blessed on my first chemo day. I pray You show me things to change and ways to love You more. And also, I pray You'd send me a song of my love for Jeremy.*

*Lord, what can I surrender to be more like You? How about my (1) pride, thinking that because You've given me strength, I occasionally forget it's all Yours. Help my pride to only be in You. How about (2) discipline, I need to learn how to diligently take all my pills, plan all healthy meals, prepare for doctor's visits and side effects, and most importantly discipline myself to put You first in my heart, day, action, thought, relationship, etc. How about (3) witnessing to non-believers. Give me a heart for all the lost! I would love for my eyes to see as You see. Then all I'd see is their hearts and You, God. Lord, how about my (4) faith? I would love to have more faith. Faith for healing, spiritual blessings, for Jeremy's faith. Faith to increase through Your Word and prayer.*

*My (5) tithing—I desire and need to be more disciplined. Forgive me for counting my Gospel for Asia Mission $ as tithing. I want to tithe to The Rock and help support it so as to give back what You've so graciously given me.*

*My (6) fear—I surrender mine for comfort. Fear of Jeremy's fear and sadness. I don't want fear. I want hope for healing and love for Jeremy and me.*

*I don't want to feel I need to please men, I only want to be an example of a child of God. I pray that all who look at my life would see that. I love Jesus and am set apart due to Your light, My God, that shines out of me! I love You!*

*Lord Jesus, I love the song that quotes Your Word, "Search me, O God, and know my heart, try me and know my anxious thoughts and see if there be any wicked way in me and lead me in the everlasting way." Jesus, I don't know what all is in me that's wicked and keeping me from all Your love, so I pray and ask You to reveal it to me so I may actively pursue changing. Jesus, I love You and praise You! Jesus, I'm thinking of the times I've been so blessed sharing what You've done in my heart this last year. You've been taking me more and more as I've chosen to surrender, thank You. Jesus, my Lord, my God, my Father, I want to give You even more. I'm so sorry for my complaining of pain, aches, comfortability, and such. It's sin, I'm sorry.*

*I want to remember truly the suffering Your love for me put You through, and I then can go through the fire if You want me to. Lord, may my heart be more like Yours in every way. May I desire what You are—Your characteristics of unconditional love, non-judgmental eyes, heart for the one lost sheep. I want to come to save the sick not the well, the poor not the rich. Jesus, I want to be like You.*

*I do pray that the doctors who misdiagnosed me long ago will correct their mistake so as to not do it again. And if it be Your will, that you would financially bless us to take care of ourselves in the future—Lord, You know I'm meaning Jeremy and me. Jesus, it's just that I feel we are already one. Now I know physically, until two are joined, that's not even an option, but in my heart, I feel it's not only You and I, Lord, it's Jeremy, too. Show me Wednesday night or Thursday day when I'm with Jeremy what Your will is. I pray he would just seek You first, fall more in love with You as You use this to bring us to our knees, and help him have his faith, hope, trust, and love in You! Lord, You're awesome. You are so incredible and so powerful, and I'm privileged to see You shine in Jeremy. I pray You'd change his heart and he would see me as a ministering trial and desire to come alongside of it. I pray his faith would know as mine knows that You, Lord, will use our lives.*

*We want to minister unto You all the days of our life and praise You, sweet Jesus. I pray Jeremy would be able to commit to loving me through the bad before the good, and that it would bring our love for You to a new level of intimacy, and our love for each other to burn strong all the days of our lives.*

*Lord, I do ask You to forgive me for thinking of him as a husband in a physical way. I know I'm called to look at him purely, and that's truly what my Spirit wants to do. Now, I know I'll have to kiss him and hold him and be held by him, but I pray through that You may be glorified. I pray Jeremy's love for me would be of what You've done in my heart, so if I'm sick this summer and do lose my hair and beauty for a time, may he still gaze upon me, and see the beauty of my Lord. And Jesus, as I look in the mirror each new day, may I not see the face that will fade away but the beauty within me that's You. I pray now that Your beauty would bless me with a poem or a song that would express the way my heart feels towards You and Jeremy. Jesus, You're worthy to be praised, and Jeremy is the one I long to love, so may this poem be from my heart, spoken of the only two men I'm in love with. Thank You for this time of waiting that You've granted me now, dear Lord; it's my love I long to set free. I praise Your name. Amen.*

*As a little girl I would sing and praise your name. But Oh, dear Lord, it seemed too often it stayed the same. Until one day You blessed me so with the man I love today by using him to say to me these few words You'll now hear me say: "Melissa, all I want to do is help you fall more in love with Christ," and with those very words You changed my life. He helped me through the hardest times I'd never thought I'd face, and yet throughout it all put a glow upon my face. Looking back, I now see how God had a mighty plan, and I am forever blessed that he used you, Jeremy Camp. No one in my life has done what you've done for me. For you've been used to help me fall more in love with my Savior. Loving the Lord and knowing His love is the greatest blessing in all my life. So, I thank you today and will so in heaven, too, for I truly believe I'm who I am mostly because of what God did through you.*

*Jeremy, I believe it's now my turn to bless you in return, with helping you to fall more in love with our Lord. So I give you my heart to love as you find more of Christ Jesus in your heart and mind. Let's serve Christ together as whatever team He wills and help show the world that there's hope still. As you've sparked in me and hopefully now I in you, let's show the world what they all wish to do. I believe with all my heart Christ has used the bad for good. For look at me today, do you feel him showing you a new way? Think of all Christ has done in this past year alone . . .*

*(Again May 22, 2000) Lord, I pray tonight (actually this morning) that Jeremy would hear my prayer and know in his heart, Melissa's loving me out there. I pray his fear for our lives would be taken away and You'd bring us together to love all our days. I long to marry him now and have him hear all the stories of how God's used this mighty man that Melissa can't wait to hold. I long for him to enjoy the love You've given me, so give us patience, dear Lord, and I pray Your will be!*

*(May 23, 2000) Dear Jesus, I just wanted to say I love You.*

# CHAPTER

## 8

# PULLED TOGETHER

*Dear Sweet Jeremy,*

*How I wish I had the perfect words to say or the most touching Scripture to share. Jeremy, I'm sorry that I don't. But what I have to give is my love. Sweetheart, I love you so much, and it's a treasure in my heart. What the Lord has done for me and continues to do is so far above all I could have ever imagined. And even though this love has a hard path to begin, I know the hard times will one day end. I want you to know this trial that I face, I don't face alone. I've prayed for you every moment of every day and will continue to. I pray the Lord will give you strength, increase your faith, and bring you joy. And I know our Lord will. I'm telling you this because you need to know my love for you is true, and I'm committed to waiting for you. If the Lord wills you another road that's separate from me, that's OK, because God's will is best for you and me. It's now my prayer that you'd let me love you. XOXO MLH*

*May 24, 2000*

*Dear Lord, the anticipation of hearing Jeremy's voice is almost too hard to handle. Lord, I'm so glad that he's coming home tonight, and I pray that You'd prepare a way for us to see each other tonight. Lord, I pray for wisdom and strength to call or wait. I'm truly needing to seek You first, and that's where my heart needs to be. Jesus, I pray for Jeremy, that You'd be with him and prepare him to see me tonight. Lord, You know how much I'm in love with Jeremy and how I long to see him every moment, so I pray that Your strength would be poured out on me and I could truly bless him. I know that it will bless Jeremy so to see me feeling healthy, so I pray tonight that could happen. Jesus, this love is so incredible, and I'm grateful every day, so I praise You and thank You.*

*Lord, I really wanted to see Jeremy tonight, and now it's too late. Well, not too late but I'll be late to church if Heather ever gets home. Lord, I'm sorry for my bad attitude, and I know I need to change. Help me see You had another plan instead for tonight and me. At least I can pray and support Jeremy as he leads the church in worship. Lord, I pray that gift You've given him would be poured out on every person listening to him tonight. I pray they would close their eyes and see You high and lifted up (Isaiah 57:15), for You live forever and Your name is Holy. May they sing, holy, holy, holy, and shine in Your light and in Your glory. Jesus, thank You for reminding me that You're first, and loving You is what I need to do first. I pray that as Jeremy is leading worship now, he would be able to concentrate on how deep and wide Your unfailing love is for him. Lord, I thank You for touching Jeremy's heart right now with enjoying Your love. I pray he'd be overflowed with peace and joy and worship. You're Almighty God.*

*Lord, I pray for Coco, too. I'm sorry I'm not able to meet up with her. It's funny how tonight is not turning out how I planned at all. But it's You, my God, who is always in control. So, even though I feel great and as healthy as can be, I'm right where You've planned me to be. I'm finally before Your face, where my heart has needed to be all the day long.*

*Lord, I love that You're in control no matter what I do, and that nothing that happens ever startles You.*

*So, I thank You for giving me more time alone with You, and now I pray You'd bless me with knowing more of You. I pray that Jeremy would boldly speak his heart, and that we'd forever, never be apart. I pray You'd always teach us the discipline we're learning now to always put You first—even when we can't see how. I pray he'd always love You 100 times more than me, and that together we would always make You happy. Jesus, I feel Your wisdom has brought me here tonight, and by that I pray Jeremy would no longer fight. I believe in faith You've spoken to his heart as You did mine, and I'm forever grateful Your work is always best. I know that no matter what he says, You've been preparing him for this day. So, dear Lord, help me hear him say... Help me always put him first, much higher than myself, and care more about him than my desire to be with him. If he loves me and commits to loving me with You, I'll be so completely blessed I don't know what I'll do. But if he knows You have another plan, I'll continue to praise Your name, and by Your grace still stand. I'm ready for whatever Your perfect will may be. So, Jesus, my dear Lord, have Your way in me and Jeremy.*

*Dear Lord, Today's Thursday, May 25th, the day Jeremy said he'd see me. And You know my heart's feeling so awkward. I feel as though the spiritual battle he's going through is so intense, and I want to pray and intercede for him. So, Lord, I lift up Jeremy to You now. I ask the lies, fears, and satanic attack would be cast away from him in Your name, Jesus. I know Your plan for Jeremy is a wonderful plan, and if it's to see me today You'll give him the strength. So, Lord, I ask he would call and come over, and that we'd be able to share this awesome healthy day together. I pray no matter what happens, that I would put him first. I do love him and care about what he's going through so very much. So I pray You'd grant me the blessing of being here for him. Jesus, help him surrender to You, knowing Your plan is always best. I surrender to You as well. No matter what the outcome, we will trust and praise You. You're so mighty, and You are the lover of my soul. So whatever You will to do, You have my life to control. Bless this day with love from You continually, so I may fall more in love with Thee. Please speak to Jeremy through Your Word and songs of praise, and help him do unto You with all of our days.*

## May 25, 2000

*Dear Lord, how can I minister to Jeremy? What can I pray or do? How can I make this road easier for him? O, Lord, he was so right when he said Ginny Owens's song was my prayer. It is, not only for me, but also for Jeremy. I know he wouldn't have chosen a life to love a woman with cancer at twenty years old. Jesus, I feel his pain, and I long to comfort him. I beg You, Jesus, to bring him here so we could talk and pray and seek Your will together. I feel my heart broken for him and me. Lord Jesus, love of my soul, help me get this love under control! I need You and Jeremy needs You, and I believe we need each other. So, Jesus, I pray for patience to wait upon You today. I pray that You'd do a work in Jeremy and bring him over today. Lord, fight this battle for him. Send angels to protect him and keep him from lies. Speak to him, Lord, I just right now called him and left a message. I pray that encourages him. I don't want him to be down in any way. I'm going to praise You and wait upon You. I love You, Lord, and trust You and Your timing.*

Jeremy did come home, but he did not immediately come over to see Melissa. After two days he came over and told her he just wanted to be her friend and that he would be there for her always and anytime she needed him. She was not discouraged. She just beamed. They went out and listened to his *Burden Me* CD in his car. She was so proud of him and loved his CD. The next day she laid in bed with Mark and me, and we all listened to it together and cried. It was so beautiful and strong—wonderful. Melissa and I wept and held each other tight.

*Dear Lord, today is Saturday, May 27, and a lot has happened in the past two days. On Thursday Jeremy came over and we talked about a lot. In fact, I see how he and I kinda switched roles in the past year. Now I'm the one who knows I'm in love with him, and he's the one who is scared and listening to everyone else. I feel when he was apologizing for kissing me, the night I told him I loved him, that he was only apologizing because his parents or friends were telling him he shouldn't have done that. Lord, I feel and know that Jeremy and I are absolutely in love, he's just so scared. Please take away his fear that I'll change my mind. Jesus, we know that's not going to ever happen! Please give him wisdom to listen to You and his heart, and not everyone else's opinion! I know it's hard to know what to do or think when everyone is telling you one thing. So, Lord, just as the time we spend together brings us closer to each other, I pray that would also happen as we spend time apart.*

*I pray Jeremy would have phenomenal faith in You that's unwavering. I pray he'd seek You and Your will and run to it, not from it.*

*I pray You'd prepare him to see me sick, and that he would grow stronger in You because of it! Lord, Thursday night was so special. I felt at the movies and even driving, even from the black thing in my tooth, we're just made for one another. I've never known a peace with anyone like I know it with You and Jeremy. Lord, this is an amazing gift, even if it's not all mine to cherish yet!*

*Lord, I feel so drawn to him in every way. This is the most amazing and unknown feeling to me. Lord, "Our God Reigns," is on the CD player, and when I hear his voice my heart jumps out of my face. I'm so blessed to love him! Thank You, Lord!*

*Jesus, I want to tell You more about Thursday. We drove around forever and talked and listened to his CD. WOW, Lord, he is so much more gifted than I ever could have imagined! It's the most awesome CD I've ever heard! I'm amazed! And I do feel I understand each song's meaning! I feel so connected to Jeremy, and I know he feels the same way. Lord, when I told him how I think so many things to say but even though I don't say them I feel he knows, he said he does. Lord, even our silence speaks love. I'm continually in awe of You while in his presence. I see Your grace, love, mercy, passion, and most of all love shining through him. It's so wonderful and beautiful. I know I will never give this mighty love and gift up. I am committed to loving Jeremy no matter what. Even if he turns his back on me and walks away, I'll never stop loving him. I know You're doing a miracle in his heart, and I will wait until it's completed!*

*O Lord, when we finally came back to the house and were sitting on the couch, I couldn't believe how much my heart, body, and soul longs for him. When my hand touched his hair and his hand my knee, I felt power flying through us. I know he has to see and feel all that I do. It was amazing how we were just pulled together. Lord, he's such an amazing man. I feel I'm about to cry just telling You about it. Lord, when we kiss, I don't feel impure or fleshed out. I feel this is my husband, and I long for the day to call him so. I know that's a lot of confidence I say this with, but Jesus I know. I know my love for Jeremy will grow each day and he will be able to see it continually blossom. I know in faith my body is healed, and You will continually bring health to my body as I work to aid You. I know in faith You'll bring Jeremy to an unwavering, committed love for me, and one day we will be married and ministering together. Jesus, prepare us for that. Prepare Jeremy to go against the odds and love me. I ask You'd change his family and friends' hearts to see the miracle You are doing in us.*

Lord Jesus, Creator of my soul, God of this earth and heaven above, King of kings and Love of my soul, Giver of peace, Master, Father, my best friend, I want to give You everything. I know this summer is and will continue to be a very hard and difficult trial upon trial! But I am committed to You, my Savior and King. No matter what it takes, I will continue to fix my eyes upon You and endure so that I may grow closer to You and the banner of love that You hold over me. I pray that Jeremy would desire to go through this hard time also, not for the glory of a trial, but to glorify You. Use my life to bring him closer to You, Jesus.

*May I rest in You, wait upon You, go when*
*You tell me to go, and stop when You say.*
*May I be so close to You that I hear*
*Your voice, love, direction, and peace in*
*everything I do and in every place I go.*

Jesus, today, You know I want to see Jeremy and call him and go with him where he goes. But I first want to go with You. Yesterday was such a lonely day—looking back I only gave You a few seconds and have learned You deserve every moment, not only a few. Change me to be more like You. I desire You, Jesus, my God and friend. I desire to be infatuated with You above and beyond that which I feel for Jeremy. I desire You! Open the eyes of my heart and my ears so I may learn more of You today in Your Word. I pray You'd give Jeremy and me boldness to see You and shine for You. Help us to always put You first, others second, and then ourselves last. May I rely on Your love, Jesus, and never on Jeremy's alone. Use him and me today wherever we go, that You may be glorified. I love You and ask that You'd help us fall more in love with You today.

*May 29, 2000*

*Dear Father, Thank You for tonight and for all the works You've begun and continue to complete. You are such an amazing God I serve! Thank You for helping Jeremy share his fears with me, now I know what more to pray for. So, Jesus, I pray You would take away his fear that I will only love him for a season and have him realize it's for a lifetime. I pray during this time right now and in our near future, I ask You to do a miracle. I pray You'd speak audibly to Jeremy, and that through Your almighty Word, and peace of prayer, he'd clearly see Your will. I thank You for giving Jeremy the wisdom to say something about our relationship. I pray You'd continue to draw us ever closer to You. I see You doing that, and I love it! I praise You, Jesus! I love You, Amen.*

*Dear Jesus, Good morning! I want to thank You so much for last night—Monday, May 29.*

*May 31, 2000*

*Jesus, I am blessed and in love with You—now more so than ever. You're so amazing! I am in awe of You and Your beauty. Jesus, as I look to the ocean, I think of You. As I see the sun peeking through the clouds, I see You. Jesus, Your beauty and Your love are too much for me to grasp. O my Almighty God, Father, Lord and King, I see You now in everything. I see You mostly in the face of the believers You've brought to me. Jesus, today was so special, more so than any other day. Today You brought Dwight to bless me. Lord I felt instantly connected to him the moment I saw him, and I thank You for bringing him to share Your love with me. When he said he's been a Christian for forty-nine years, all I could think was how beautiful to know You and love You that long. Jesus, I instantly saw You shining through Dwight's face, and it was beautiful. The love and humility he had, the boldness yet gentleness, the strength yet compassion. Jesus, I loved that! I loved him speaking of his beautiful, wonderful wife, Ruth. How much love he has for her; and when he spoke of his children, especially his thirty (some year old) daughter. How he said she married a pastor and is beautiful. When he walked away, I felt the charge of extra love given by You to us both through the tears we shared while saying goodbye. The blessing of him saying I'm like his daughter was a treasured gift.*

*Lord, You are so kind and so loving! I do love You more than anything and anyone. I love every light You've created that reminds me of You. I love every noise from nature that reminds me of You. I love the beauty of grass rolling into this lake that reminds me of You! You are my King! You are the lover of my soul! Jesus, You make me whole. O Father, I love You. What would You have me ask for now? Or what would You desire to say to me? As high as the heavens above, so is the height of My love; as deep as the ends of the sea, so is your love for me.*

"Arms of grace and love, that's what awaits you, My love. This is more than you would plan, but take comfort in My hand patiently guiding you each step of the way. I will never leave you to fall or stray. My hand is holding you up, my dear child, do not think it's your strength. Be humble, be meek, and always seek Me, *the Lord of your life. Be patient, be strong, trust in Me alone. Wait in earnest expectancy, constantly giving glory to Me.* "

Okay, Jesus, I have a few things I need to say. Dwight told me of many wonderful things today. First, he said how he went to the restroom, and while walking out began to pray and ask You for a personal ministry once again. And then there he saw me sitting with You. When he approached me, I immediately was comforted by the bond of love we shared for You. Jesus, thank You! Thank You for this dear old man. Thank You for his faithfulness to come and sit with me. When he shared this story, I felt changed. . . .

Dwight had a dear friend who thought he was catching a cold, and yet found out he had fallen sick with cancer. This man, young in his thirties, began to get very sick. So Dwight went to see him at his mothers-in-law's, where he was resting in a hospital bed. When Dwight saw him, he was very ill, and Dwight had to lean down to his face and speak into this man's ear. This man loved the Lord dearly, and was and is an incredible person. So, as he talked to him, Dwight asked how he was doing. The man told him he was depressed and began to explain why. He said he was depressed because a few weeks ago he had gone into the presence of the Lord, "passing away to You for a short time." And he said the grace and the love was so powerful and embracing. Dwight and I began to cry at this moment. Then he said he felt, this is it, I'm home. Then You, Jesus, told him he had to go back. Your love is so huge that this sick man was able to see Your presence and hear You tell him to go back because a certain man he knew was not yet saved. So, this man was depressed to have had to leave home, leave You, Jesus. You are our home.

And I thank You for Your grace allowing us to live here each day to be used by You and help bring others into salvation, until the glorious day when You call us home. My Jesus, I praise You for that dear man Dwight told me of, and I thank You he is at home with You now. My spirit wants to go home. O, how I long to be home. But I also long for more here on Earth. I ask You to extend my life so I may impact others as You continually impact my life through Your faithful servants.

Jesus, I want to praise You now more than ever. I pray for a continual humbling to be upon my life. I ask You to strip me of my pride, ever-so-gently.

*I pray You would use my life to show the world how mighty You are! You are so amazing and will do so many wonderful things through my life until the day You've completed the work You've planned to do and call me into Your throne of grace and love to embrace me!*

Jesus, You know all the desires of my heart. You know how I desire to love You first, to be used to bring You glory continually all my days long. You know how I desire to fulfill the ministry You've called me to. I desire to be used through my chemotherapy. I desire to be a miracle. I desire to be humbled, yet I desire to be the miracle chemo patient whose hair is held in by JESUS. I desire to love Jeremy Camp all the days of my long life. I desire to marry him and minister with him, to help him in every way I can. I desire to live a bold life, knowing You more each day.

Teach me Your ways, O Lord. Have me delight in You, be my treasure, and in Your way through Your will may You give me my heart's desire. May Your grace abound more and Your love more. May I be a light that shines for You. Use my gift tonight at the Bible Study. I pray for eyes to *hear Your Word and eyes to see anyone You may have planned for me to talk to. Open or close my mouth to the group as You will. Bless the worship—Jeremy and the guys—that we may all intimately worship and love You. I love You, Jesus, more than life. So I give You my life as a small gift for this great love. Thank You for loving me. I love You! I love You! I love You! Amen.*

*Lord Jesus, I pray through the power of Your Holy Spirit that my faith in You and Your power would increase. I pray knowing that You have the power to heal and to save. What a beautiful and awesome God I serve! O Jesus, I pray now through all faith, knowing I am healed in the power of Your name, Jesus. I pray all the lies and doubts I have from the devil would be cast away in Your name, Jesus. I know You desire to use my life, and You know I desire to give it. Jesus, You are incredible! Absolutely incredible, and I am in awe of You. So in faith I ask You to use this chemotherapy to kill all microscopic cancer cells in my body. I also pray all fast-growing good cells to remain intact! Jesus, You delight in healing, and I delight in You. So, Lord, I pray, believing You can and will, if You choose, use your power to answer my prayer. I ask Your hand would hold in the hairs of my head, that not even one would fall out. I pray I would not get sick or even notice pain. I ask that I may deny myself and put others first.*

*Lord, use me in the cancer ward and with anyone you chose. Delight in my life, for I delight in You. Jesus, please pray for me. There are so many things going on and to come that I don't know what I ought to pray. So I ask for discernment to know what to pray for. Jesus, may my faith ever increase, no matter what's to come. I pray also for the gift of compassion. Lord, I don't want to look at a group of believers and think I need to minister to them all. I want to minister to whom You want me to and allow those to minister to me whom You desire to. Jesus, use my life and Jeremy's to please You. We desire to bring You gladness. I love You and praise You for the miracles You have planned and for the good work You've begun in me. Jesus, You're awesome. Bring us into Your throne of grace and love that we may hear You. I pray You'd help me listen more to Jeremy and be there for him. Bless him today with Your presence and love. Bring him joy in these trials.*

*"Who delivered us from so great a death, and does deliver us; in whom we trust that He will still deliver us, you also helping together in prayer for us, that thanks may be given by many persons on our behalf for the gift granted to us through many"*

—2 CORINTHIANS 1:10-11

*"fellow workers for your joy; for by faith you stand."*

—2 CORINTHIANS 1:24

*Melissa, talk to Jeremy about the fear you have that you know is stupid and a lie, but that he's excited to get married and that maybe not realizing it's me he wants to marry. Jesus, take this stupid fear away but help me open up and tell Jeremy. I pray in the power of the name of Jesus that Your name would rebuke Satan from me and the lies in my head.*

*Dear Sweet Lord,*
*Today is June 4, Grandma's birthday, and it's been a while since I talked (wrote) to You about Jeremy. I'm sorry I've been doing so many other things than writing and truly giving You all my attention. So, Jesus, my sweet Jesus, I pray tonight as I sleep, I may get the rest my body needs and put You first tomorrow and always. I thank You for increasing my love for Jeremy every day, and I pray my love for You would do the same. I love You and pray You'd bless Jeremy tonight with sleep and rest, peace and joy of You through You, and likewise with me. I love you, Amen.*

*Dear Jesus, Today is a new day that I believe will be hard. I'm realizing my hair is definitely thinning out. So, my sweet Jesus, prepare me for anything and everything! I desire Your will to be done and for You, My God, to be glorified. Help me rely upon Your love through the storms and through the rain, like the sun shining down from above. I rely upon Your love. Teach me Your Word today, that I may know and love You more! Jesus, I love You. Be now my vision and be now glorified.*

*Reaffirm your love for him; our sufficiency is from God—the Spirit gives life.*

*"But we have this treasure in earthen vessels, that the excellence of the power may be of God and not of us. We are hard-pressed on every side, yet not crushed; we are perplexed, but not in despair; persecuted, but not forsaken; stuck down, but not destroyed—always carrying about in the body the dying of the Lord Jesus, that the life of Jesus also may be manifested in our body. For we who live are always delivered to death for Jesus' sake, that the life of Jesus also may be manifested in our mortal flesh."—2 Corinthians 4:7-11*

*"Walk by faith, not by sight."—2 Corinthians 5:7*

*"We are confident, yes, well pleased rather to be absent from the body and to be present with the Lord."—2 Corinthians 5:8*

*Thank You, Jesus, that one day soon You'll call us home to be in Your Almighty presence forever!*

*"Therefore we make it our aim, whether present or absent, to be well pleasing to Him."—2 Corinthians 5:9*

*Lord, may I not take pride in external things (like 2 Corinthians 5:12). I desire to boast in the eternal working of Your glory!*

*Melissa, now that you live, remember Christ died for you and for all, so if He died for all then, you should live no longer for yourself, but for Him who died for you and rose again (2 Corinthians 5:15).*

*June 7, 2000*

*Dear sweet Jesus, how awesome are Your works, O Lord. How great and mighty are Your plans. I thank You that each day I'm blessed to learn more and more of Your almighty love. So many things I wanted to do and many things I should have, but You still love me—no matter what, Lord. I know Your love isn't based on my actions, my works, or anything I do. Simply knowing this is beautiful. Lord, how unworthy I am to be loved this way, yet so completely grateful. Jesus, Your love truly is all that I need. All I need is You! Lord, I do thank You that You have chosen to bless me with the blessing of loving Jeremy and him loving me. This love is high above my dreams. I want to write this Scripture Jeremy shared with me— our Scripture.*

*"For this reason I bow my knees to the Father of our Lord Jesus Christ, from whom the whole family in heaven and earth is named, that He would grant you, according to the riches of His glory, to be strengthened with might through His Spirit in the inner man, that Christ may dwell in your hearts through faith; that you, being rooted and grounded in love, may be able to comprehend with all the saints what is the width and length and depth and height— to know the love of Christ which passes knowledge; that you may be filled with all the fullness of God.*

*Now to Him who is able to do exceedingly abundantly above all that we ask or think, according to the power that works in us, to Him be glory in the church by Christ Jesus to all generations, forever and ever. Amen."*

—EPHESIANS 3:14-21

*"Behold, I tell you a mystery: We shall not all sleep, but we shall all be changed—in a moment, in the twinkling of an eye, at the last trumpet. For the trumpet will sound, and the dead will be raised incorruptible, and we shall be changed."*

—1 CORINTHIANS 15:51-52

*"Therefore, my beloved brethren, be steadfast, immovable, always abounding in the work of the Lord, knowing that your labor is not in vain in the Lord."*

—1 CORINTHIANS 15:58

*"who comforts us in all our tribulation, that we may be able to comfort those who are in any trouble, with the comfort with which we ourselves are comforted by God."*

—2 Corinthians 1:4

*Dear sweet Jesus, how I've thought to write You so many times, and yet haven't. I'm sorry. Jesus, I thank You that I can pray or write, cry or whisper, and that You hear me. You're so awesome! Jesus, I want to go back to the day Jeremy told me he loved me, too! I want to write down all my emotions and what happened. Let me start the night before Tuesday night.*

*Jesus, I remember going to the Bible Study and wondering how it was going to be. Because for me I felt I could announce to everyone how I am in love with Jeremy, but I knew he wasn't quite there yet. Funny how I always knew he'd be ready someday. I remember when I parked, I saw Aaron and Christy walking down the hill. I'm so glad I caught up with them that night, because as soon as I did, we saw Jeremy and some guy talking outside. Lord, it was so special, it reminded me of when Jeremy first liked me, and I could tell through the unspoken words of his actions. When he greeted the girls, he shook their hand and then hugged me. Lord, it meant so much to me. You know Jeremy has always stood apart from every other man. Thank You, Jesus. I remember feeling kinda irritated, I wanted to be able to be with Jeremy but at the same time allow him the freedom to talk with others and be with others without feeling trapped by me. Jesus, I bet it was funny looking down at Jeremy and me. It's like the two of us are so drawn to each other and communicating with You the entire time about how hard it is to not know what to do. I'm so glad that's over now.*

*But back to the story. During worship I felt nothing in the world mattered, not how I sounded or anyone else, but all that mattered was You, Lord. I've always felt Jeremy leads me into the throne like no other. After the study began, Heather came in and sat up by Jeremy near the front door. I looked up at them during the prayer because I heard them laughing quietly together, and it was so fun to see. The prayer was like fifteen minutes long because of the way Mike was leading the Bible Study, and very quiet—silent praying. It was just so awesome to see them together. I was looking up at two of the people I loved most in this world. Yes, I love my entire family the same, but to see Heather with Jeremy, and smiling, too, was a treat beyond measure. Lord, I have to say that being in love makes me so sappy. I notice my heart flowing out of my mouth in poetic psalm like words. In many ways, I love it.*

*Back to Tuesday night, after the study I started talking to Jeremy as he was playing guitar, and while I was talking to him, I noticed many other girls around. I was thinking I shouldn't stand here by him because maybe he doesn't feel comfortable talking to me in front of his roommate. So I got him and myself some water, and in just the few moments I was gone, other girls had gathered around him. So I handed the water to someone to give him and figured if he wanted to talk to me, he would come up to me. It was hard, because all I wanted to do was talk with him and be with him, but it's not how it worked out. I ended up talking to Natalie for a long time, and Jeremy talked to Sarah. Then, after it was over, I went outside and Jeremy, Sarah, and Natalie were all out there. It was kinda cute but awkward. All I wanted was to pull him aside and say, "I love you, let's talk."*

*I could tell something was wrong with him, but I didn't know if it was me. So we all went into my car to listen to Jeremy's CD, because we were dying to hear it. It was so amazing. I remember hearing his song "Letting Go" and having it pierce my heart. I even looked into Jeremy's eyes and quoted the line about letting go of pain and fears. He said his music speaks to his heart as well. Lord, hearing that song reminded me of how far You have brought Jeremy and me.*

*I'm saying this because I remember coming home one night and Jeremy and Ryan were downstairs. All I wanted to do was be with them, yet I felt I was still holding on to my fickle feelings for Jeremy, and that they were best held up inside my heart. So, when I finally did go downstairs and Jeremy began playing that same song, "Letting Go," I felt You, Lord, telling me to let Jeremy go. I'll never forget how hard that was. I remember walking away in so much pain. I even remember how it felt to go up the stairs to my room. Lord, it was so hard. As soon as I got into my room, I fell to my knees and cried out to You, Lord. It's so weird how I felt you telling me to let Jeremy go. I've never felt more pain. I was drawn to my knees through tears, and yet drawn to be downstairs by Jeremy. I even remember the door was slightly cracked open, and for some reason I felt his presence even closer, it was like all we had between us was the door to my room, and yet that was so much.*

*But back to the night in the car. After we listened, we all laughed and had a good time until I said an unhumorous sarcasm to Jeremy and hurt his feelings. I felt so bad, because I didn't intend to hurt him. I was just playing off his joke of how I'm overdramatic when I try to be funny. But unfortunately, I hurt him even to the point where he got out of the car. I'm being stupid thinking he's tired and annoyed. I think he just wants to go, and he's probably thinking I'm just mean. I get in the car to drive away and feel terrible. I don't want to drive away, but I feel Jeremy doesn't want me near him. So I was slowly starting up the car and praying to You, then he came near the car. Thank You, Lord, for his soft heart to never let me go in a weird mood or in an uncomfortable way. He's always so great to mend anything. I pray we would be like this forever! Jesus, that night talking, we spoke of so many things. I thought it so dear when he said "walk me through this, Melissa;" it was so cute. Jeremy is so cute. I just wanted to hold his hand and say I love you and know I'll love you tomorrow; I loved you always and always will continue to love you. But I held back most of that and held his hand and tried to walk him through it. The only bad thing was I was exhausted and felt like many of the things I was saying were dumb. But it didn't matter, because even through my rambling mouth and open ears, God worked mightily, showing Jeremy and me how much we do care and love each other.*

*Jeremy later told me that night when he went home to bed, he finally could sleep and that when he woke up, he knew he loved me. It's funny, Lord, because I think sometimes our spirit knows something all along and yet our mind takes a while to accept and know it, too. My love for Jeremy has been growing since the day I met him, and all the while my spirit knew but my mind and heart were not accepting it. Thank You, Lord, for allowing me to accept this now. You're so gracious and patient to do a mighty work so that Jeremy and I may love one another all the more! Jesus, Jeremy later told me that the next Wednesday morning, he woke up and knew he loved me, and that in the right timing he would tell me. Well, the right timing was going to be when I was ready—when Jeremy could see that I not only needed to be strong for him but could be weak. He thought this would take like six months or something. Instead, God chose to work fast and speedily, and by that night we were planning our future together as man and wife. Lord, You're so good and awesome. These past two weeks without him have been a major learning point through trial and error. And all I want to say is I love You.*

*Jesus, to finish the story, Jeremy and I are not like any other couple I know. Instead of him asking me to marry him, things went like this:*

*That night I had gone running, and then stopped by Sarah and Natalie's for a little while. It's funny how on my way home, I knew Jeremy would be at the house. It wasn't a surprise at all to see his car when I pulled up. But it definitely was wonderful. So I walked in the house only to see the most awesome thing. Jeremy was sitting on the couch with Ryan, reading him Scripture. I love how Jeremy is so bold for the Lord and Ryan gleans from it. I sat down with them for a little while, and then Ryan realized he had lost his keys. This began an hour of endless searching for Ryan's missing keys. I wanted to help and all, but after an hour had passed, I was ready to be alone with Jeremy. We even left and came back and continued to look for the keys. So, finally I asked Jeremy if he would want to go outside with me for a little bit. So we walked outside and stood by Ryan's truck. I was feeling pretty awkward all night, and finally told Jeremy as best as I could describe it. I said, "I'm feeling weird." He knew, and told me that I didn't need to be strong for him; that I could tell him anything.*

*That was all I needed to hear, because God used that to aid me in pouring out my heart filled with fears and doubts, and surrender them to God. I told Jeremy the fears I even held back from God, because I felt it would mean I had a lack of faith if I admitted them. But somehow God knew I needed to share this and couldn't without the help and love from Jeremy. It was so beautiful to me, realizing God broke my fear down, and I guess it was beautiful to Jeremy too, because he held me weeping in his arms, and he said the words I loved to hear. He said, "I love You, too!" I looked up to God and said I love you so much. Jeremy said, "I've always loved you." Then we both wept together for the first time as one. How precious that moment will forever remain in my memory. I'll soon forget the chaos of the lost keys, Tyler and Megan coming home in the middle of our conversation, and the locksmith who came and broke into Ryan's car.*

> All those things I'll forget, and soon all I'll remember is that Jeremy helped me in the hardest time of my life, and then as if that wasn't enough, decided to walk through my life with me.

Melissa and Jeremy stayed up almost all night discussing their wedding and their life together. They were so excited. Melissa rushed up the stairs in the morning to tell all! God is so good, and all His ways are good and kind.

Over the next few days, Melissa began to say to Jeremy, "Hey, you never really asked me to marry you!" With that hint, Jeremy brought over a large, beautiful bouquet of roses and got down on one knee and proposed to her in front of me and her dad as we took pictures. Prayers are answered and dreams do come true!

The one thing Jeremy didn't have was a ring. My mother had given me her diamond ring, and I wanted Melissa to have it. I knew she would love it, and it would have sentimental value to her because she had a very special relationship with her grandma. I talked to Mom about it, and we both loved the idea. After some discussion of Melissa wanting me to have it because I had lost my diamond years ago, and our insistence that we wanted her to have it, it was settled. It gave Grandma and me so much happiness when I presented Jeremy and Melissa with a diamond ring that they could have set to their liking. The two of them had so much fun shopping for a setting for the ring. They chose the perfect one for Melissa—a platinum solitaire with a 1-carat diamond.

Melissa was beyond blessed and excited about becoming Mrs. Jeremy Camp. In her bliss, she began thinking about her dad, and how hard it must be for him to see his little girl sick with cancer and now giving her care over to another man. She sat down and wrote him a note:

> *Thank you for every memory and special day you gave. Thank you for your hugs, smiles, and tears. Thank you for blessing me with the family that we share, but more than anything, I thank you for placing me in God's care. I love my Lord so very much, and it all began with your tender love. Daddy, you have always been and forever will be the first man who taught me of my heavenly Daddy. So never doubt or even think you haven't been tremendous to me! You were in my eyes an amazing man who loved and lived for Jesus, and you are still that today. Because of your heart, I searched for one alike, and thanks to you, Dad, I'm marrying a man of God, too! I love you.*

Was it difficult for Mark? Yes and no. Yes, because as her earthly father he felt an overwhelming responsibility to take care of this child that he loved so much. No, because he knew that he was not in control—only their heavenly Father was. He trusted Him and would walk by faith. He would be the man Melissa needed, a man who loved and lived for Jesus. Mark also loved Jeremy. He knew him, and he never doubted that God had chosen him to walk alongside of Melissa through her cancer and throughout her life.

The month of May was a whirlwind. It was filled with great sorrow and great joy. We saw the glory of the Lord shinning within Melissa, and we saw His faithfulness to her in giving her the desires of her heart.

Melissa seemed to joyfully fly through chemotherapy. She would still run along the beach and continued ministering the love of Jesus to everyone she could. Jeremy was often away touring, but when he was home, he would stay on a mattress downstairs in our family room so he could be close to Melissa and take care of her.

I would continue to take her to her chemo appointments, and she loved being able to talk to all the other cancer patients. Of course, I wanted to stay with her. I never wanted to leave her so I could make sure she was being cared for. But after the first session, Melissa insisted she could minister better if I left. This was her ministry, and I needed to allow her to shine in it without me there.

Melissa had anti-nausea medication that worked great, so she was rarely sick. We did have one incident of sickness in the car right after a chemo treatment. I pulled the car into a restaurant parking lot and started cleaning up while her little sister Megan comforted her. Of course, Melissa was apologetic and didn't want me to have to clean it up—my sweet girl.

The one thing she really wanted and prayed for was for her hair not to fall out. She had beautiful, long, chestnut-colored hair. She loved her hair. I loved her hair! But the day came exactly as the doctor said—eleven days after chemo started, her hair began to fall out. She got her Dad's electric razor and went in our bathroom alone. She didn't want anyone watching. She shaved her head, or attempted to do so, with much frustration. The razor was not intended to handle her long hair and would jam and stop working, but she stuck with it. After a long time, she exited the bathroom more beautiful than any other day of her life. She was even more gorgeous without hair! You could see the lovely, delicate shape of her head and her beautiful features more clearly. Her eyes, her smile, her countenance, all were enhanced. She still wasn't confident in showing anyone, even though we told her she was gorgeous. That night her brother also shaved his head so he could show his love and support for her. Megan told her she was going to shave her head also. Melissa said to her and her many friends who also wanted to shave their heads, "No you're not! I don't want to be looking at a bunch of bald people!"

Melissa gathered an array of cute hats and bandanas, but no scarves. She was always fashionable and just couldn't handle the look of chemo scarves. Her grandparents wanted to buy her a wig, thinking that would help her, so off we went to shop and try on wigs. We bought one, but she hated it and wore it maybe twice. Back to bandanas and hats, cute as could be!

The amazing month of May taught us so much about the character of God and gave us great hope for Melissa and Jeremy's future. Melissa flooded the pages of her journals with love songs, prayers, and details of God working to pull together these two anointed children of His. He had a great purpose and plan for their lives that was unseen to them but known in Melissa's heart. She expected the miraculous; she expected God to do exceedingly, abundantly, above all she could ask or think! Melissa and Jeremy's life together had begun.

*Lord Jesus, I praise You for this love given to us by You. We know that every good and perfect gift is from You, so we thank You. And now I ask that You'd help us fall more in love with You, as we are together and falling more in love with each other. Lord, You are so above being worthy of our praise, but to be able to praise You, I'll thank You for, for all eternity. I ask now that You'd humble us continually by Your presence, that Jeremy and I would always be reminded "it's all about You, Jesus." Be magnified, glorified, and praised through our lives of love to You. In You I hope, and in You we rest. Amen.*

# CHAPTER
## 9

# MIRACLES DO HAPPEN

*J*eremy did not want to wait to get married. He knew Melissa was his wife, and both decided they wanted to get married sooner than later. He was very vocal to all of us, "I want to go through this with her as her husband."

So we began to plan. They picked October 21, 2000, for their wedding. That was less than five months away! Melissa had such joy in planning, and so did I. Bridal magazines, folders, pictures, organizing, and wedding dress shopping filled our days. She loved every minute of planning their wedding. And I couldn't say no to anything they wanted. I had no idea how we were going to pull off a huge wedding, but they wanted everyone they knew or ever met to be there. They wanted the world to share in their joy and all that God had done in their lives. How do you say no to that?

One of our great joys during this season was shopping for a wedding dress. Jeremy was adamant: "no strapless dresses." Melissa was equally concerned about being modest and elegant. She had a dress that she had pictured in her mind, and she was going to find it. We hit every store in San Diego, and some in Orange County as well. Melissa was so fun. She was game for trying on every style and played dress up just like when she was a little girl. In those early years she often would change her clothes five times a day! We laughed hysterically at the ball gown that swallowed up her tiny frame and cringed at other styles that looked ridiculous, if that is even possible on such a beautiful girl. Finally we found the dress that matched her vision—oh happy day!

But as we were planning a wedding, we were still keenly aware we were fighting cancer. We focused on nutrition and dietary supplements that were recommended for cancer patients. We researched, read, and obtained advice.

*Lord it's been a while since I've written to You, and yet so much has happened. Lord, I've learned how worthy You are to be praised, and yet I know I have still not seen the majesty of Your glory. Lord, You are so good, and I love You more than anything this world could offer. My Jesus, I pray that You would look into Jeremy's and my heart and see that our hearts are set after You. Lord, I look to the Scripture You've given Jeremy and me separately and together during this trial and victory.*

*"Now to Him who is able to do exceedingly abundantly above all that we ask or think, according to the power that works in us, to Him be glory in the church by Christ Jesus to all generations, forever and ever. Amen."*

— *Ephesians 3:20-21*

Checkup day came. Melissa had finished her round of chemotherapy. She had a sonogram and other tests that were needed to check on the success of the chemo, and then it was time to meet with her doctor for the results. We were expecting good news. She looked great and was feeling great. Melissa, me, her dad, Ryan, Megan, Heather, and Jeremy crowded into an exam room and waited. Heather was holding my hand, and as the wait became longer and longer, she began squeezing my hand harder and harder. My fingers were becoming numb. Good news did not take this long! The doctor finally came in and was very somber. He told Melissa that the new sonogram revealed another 4-centimeter tumor on her other ovary. He said it looked identical to the first cancerous tumor, and the radiologist was certain it also was cancerous. We needed to see Dr. Koonings and schedule surgery. We were stunned and in a fog.

Melissa, Jeremy, and I got in to see Dr. Koonings immediately. He told Melissa she would need a complete hysterectomy as soon as possible. This was two months before their wedding, but surgery could not wait. Melissa asked if she could talk to Dr Koonings by herself, so Jeremy and I went out to the waiting room.

I was devastated for Melissa, but also very concerned for Jeremy. I could only imagine what he was going through. First, he must deal with the fact that the woman he loved had cancer. Then he was faced with the news that she now must have a hysterectomy. They both love children; I knew he wanted a family.

I asked him, "Are you OK?"

He said to me, "I am so OK—God has prepared me my whole life for this, and **I consider it an honor that God has chosen me to go through this with Melissa.**"

WOW! I love Jeremy. I was blessed, overwhelmed, and in awe by his love for my daughter. God is so amazing! He blessed us greatly with this incredible young man to help carry us through our darkest hours. His faith gave mine strength. I have never been as proud of anyone as I was of Jeremy in that moment.

The surgery was scheduled. Melissa and Jeremy were prepared and walking by faith. Both were steadfast, praying for healing and trusting God with the results. There was no doubting, whining, complaining, or anger with God. He was too real to them—they knew Him! They had joy in His strength. They rejoiced in His salvation. He had given them their heart's desire; He had answered so many of their prayers. He met them with the blessings of goodness and made them exceedingly glad with His presence. I could see Psalm 21 being played out in their lives, and I was in awe of God and both Melissa and Jeremy.

*I have faith You can heal my womb and protect me and bless me one day with children that I may raise to worship and love You. Oh, no matter if my womb is barren or blessed, I will help bring children into a deep love and adoration for You!*

The morning of her surgery, an associate pastor came to see Melissa in the pre-op room. He prayed a powerful prayer for healing, and both Melissa and Jeremy felt something unexplainable happen. There was no big prayer meeting, no celebrity pastor, just this one humble man.

We were told the surgery would last five hours. After Lis was taken back to the operating room, Jeremy left to go and call his family. Mark also left to make phone calls to keep everyone informed. Heather was exhausted and went into the chapel and lay down on a pew. I paced back and forth in front of the waiting room. I had waited here before; I was very familiar with this corridor, the section between the waiting room and the operating room doors that had the big picture windows looking out over the parking lot to the small church with the cross. I paced and prayed and reflected again on the cross. Jesus was there with us. We are called to the fellowship of His suffering. He's in control. As I reflected on these truths, I thought I was at peace. I felt strong and confident. But I was not leaving that corridor.

Then I heard, "Henning." It startled me. It had only been one and a half hours. I looked in the waiting room and saw Dr. Koonings standing in the doorway of the bad news room. He called my name, "Janette." I was overcome with horror. Grief and sorrow overwhelmed me. I rushed to him and threw my arms around his neck just to hang on to someone. My legs were weak and could hardly support me. I was weeping—loudly. I thought Melissa must have died. The surgery was to last five hours, not one and a half. Dear Heather, who was in the chapel next to the waiting room, could hear me weeping and came rushing in. Dr. Koonings kept saying, "Janette, it's OK. There was nothing there. I opened her up and there was no tumor—nothing at all." WHAT? I couldn't comprehend what he was saying. He had to repeat it several times. I said, "It's gone? Is it a miracle?" He, equally surprised and confused, said, "Yes, there was a 4-centimeter dense cancerous tumor there yesterday, and now there is nothing." My only thought was that I had to find Jeremy and tell him.

I ran out of the waiting room towards the elevator. Jeremy was just coming off, and I began to yell down the corridor, "Jeremy, she's healed, she's healed!" It seemed like I was running in slow motion, trying to get to him to tell him the miraculous news. Finally I reached Him, and we hugged and cried. He began running back and forth with joy and awe. He fell to his knees in front of the big picture window that looked out to the cross, raised his hands to the Lord, and prayed and praised Him, all the while crying tears of joy. The entire waiting room and corridor were filled with people, all of them seeing and hearing about Melissa's miracle.

When they wheeled Melissa out from the operating room and down our corridor, we rushed over to her. She was glowing—like an angel, I thought. Jeremy leaned down to her and told her that God had healed her—there was no tumor. She reached up her arms and grabbed ahold of his neck and pulled him down to her face. With tears streaming down her face, she said, "Oh, that God would do this for me!" She continued to hold Jeremy by the neck all the way to her room while her brother leaned down on the other side of the bed. When she got to her room, Melissa prayed the most spirit-filled prayer I have ever heard. Everyone in the room was in awe—the presence of God was so real. A nurse came in to do what nurses must do after you're back from surgery. She was one of the detached ones, just doing her job. Melissa reached out to her and held her arm and said, "Do you believe in God?" Then Melissa proceeded to tell her what had just happened. After she slightly recovered, she asked for the phone. She had to call the Stones and tell them what happened. They were the first people she called.

That was a glorious day. Melissa's little sister Megan and Sam her friend recorded a message on our answering machine. They sang, "We believe in miracles!"

Dr. Koonings came and sat down on the bed to tell Melissa what happened. She asked him specifically if it was a miracle. He told her he had no other explanation for it. He then said that he took some deep tissue biopsies so they could see if there were any microscopic cancer cells there. Melissa was joyful and grateful for the miracle, but expressed to me her concerns about the biopsies.

The biopsy reports came back, and there were indeed microscopic cancer cells in her liver. What did that mean? What do we do now? Dr. Koonings told Melissa and Jeremy to go and get married. Enjoy your honeymoon! Have babies! He gave them hope that they could have a normal life together, and that they could have children. They put the concern of microscopic cancer cells out of their minds and began to live life as an engaged, happy couple planning their wedding.

Melissa absolutely loved ministering with Jeremy. She would go with him when he played worship at different churches and helped him sell his CDs. She was living out her answered prayer—ministering with Jeremy, becoming his wife. She was able to give her testimony at an amphitheater during one of his concerts and share not just about God healing her, but the amazing work of salvation in her life. They were touching people's lives together—always looking for the "one" God had chosen for them to tell His story to.

# CHAPTER 10

# THE WEDDING

*W*ith a great deal of joy and faith, the wedding planning was in full gear. It was a joyous time, and God provided for every desire of Melissa's heart. The exact wedding dress she had in her mind. Eleven bridesmaids with blush pink and white dresses. Six hundred handmade invitations. Flowers, food, plus all the help needed to pull it off in such a short time.

One thing that she was concerned about was her hair. It was growing back, but very slowly. Jeremy told her she was beautiful and he loved her hair. He even helped her figure out a cute hairstyle. We had trouble finding a veil and a headpiece that would fit her. We finally found a pearl headband that she loved, but we needed a veil. One day we were shopping, and we walked into a wedding dress store in the mall. As we walked in, we could hear Jeremy's music coming from the speakers in the store. I began looking at veils, and the owner of the store began to talk to me. I asked about Jeremy's music, and she told me she went to Horizon Christian Fellowship and had heard the news about Jeremy and Melissa and has been praying for them. I said, "Well, there they are!" She met them both and told Melissa she would love to make her a veil that would look beautiful with her headband, and that it was her gift to them! God's hand was everywhere and in every detail.

Over six hundred people attended the wedding. Mark and I walked Melissa down the aisle. She had the biggest smile and was overjoyed at seeing Jeremy waiting for her. Mark prayed a beautiful prayer for them, then gave our daughter away to a man of faith whom we trusted with our most precious of all gifts—our daughter Melissa. Many people have asked us how we could do that. She was so young, and she had cancer. How could we give life-or-death decision-making power over to Jeremy, who was only twenty-two? Why not wait until she was better? People love to ask questions and give opinions.

The answer was easy for Mark and me. We had gone to the Lord in prayer and settled this question months before. The answer was the same; we trusted God, we trusted Jeremy, we loved Jeremy. Most importantly, Melissa and Jeremy loved each other. I've never seen two people love each other like they did. But even more than all that, we had watched the hand of God moving in all our lives. We knew God's hand was upon Melissa and Jeremy, and that God still had an amazing work He was doing. We were on the sidelines watching as His plan unfolded. It was undeniable that God was in the process of doing something beyond our comprehension at the time. We weren't about to get in His way.

The wedding was a celebration of love both for each other and their love for Jesus. As they walked up to the altar, the name of Jesus was prominently written for all to see. It was perfect—the name of Jesus written like a banner over them, covering them with His love. Jeremy sang a song he had written to Melissa; they sang songs of love to each other and worshiped the Lord, and they spoke traditional vows of "for better, for worse, for richer, for poorer, in sickness and in health, until death do us part." Melissa looked out to all the guests with a huge smile, drawing them in and scooping them up into her joy. I was told that many felt the presence of God, and some even thought the Rapture would happen at any moment. It was a very special day.

We were all filled with joy and hope. Melissa was feeling great. There was no outward sign of illness. We had put our fears into the Lord's hands and believed there was a beautiful future ahead for them.

Melissa and Jeremy headed off on their honeymoon. They were able to go to the north shore of Oahu in Hawaii. They stayed at Melissa's aunt's house on Sunset Beach and had a dream honeymoon for two weeks. They had so much fun, with lots of love, goofiness, and laughter. Melissa loved showing Jeremy around the island that she loved so much, a place she had stayed many times, a place where she had written in her journals while she prayed and dreamed of her husband. It was a place of beauty—paradise—a place where we always felt like heaven actually touches Earth.

Jeremy had taken along his guitar, and he worked on finishing up his song "Walk By Faith." Melissa loved helping him figure out the right words that would go together. She loved singing with him, and he loved teaching her harmony.

After two weeks in Hawaii, they went to Indiana to celebrate with Jeremy's family and friends from back home. I went to the airport to pick them up when they returned. They had been gone for three weeks. The moment I saw Melissa, I knew something was wrong. It was the first time I saw her looking really sick—thin and pale. It scared me, but I tried not to show it.

When they got home, Jeremy was excited to play and sing his song "Walk By Faith." As he played the song and got to the lyric,

> I will walk by faith even when I cannot see, because this broken road prepares Your will for me,

Melissa leaned over and whispered to me, "I thought of those words, Mom." She was so delighted that she was able to help him with this amazing song. I thought about Melissa's broken road, knowing God had prepared His perfect path for her.

They had arranged to stay at a guest house of some dear friends in Rancho Santa Fe while they continued to look for an apartment. Melissa and I searched, and I found an apartment in Carlsbad down by the beach. The one thing she really wanted was a laundry room inside the apartment. These apartments were new construction and affordable. We walked into the unit to preview it, then I heard a scream of joy. Melissa had opened a closet in the bathroom, and to her great delight there was a laundry room! This was it! Again, the Lord was giving her the desires of her heart.

Melissa was beginning to feel pain, and her abdomen was swollen. She showed me her tummy and said, "Mom, maybe I'm pregnant." I asked her a few questions and concluded that she was not pregnant. She thought maybe she was eating too much. No, not that either. She made an appointment to see Dr. Koonings. I did not go with them—it was the first appointment that I missed. They were married now, and I needed to let them fly solo, or at least that was my thinking.

While Melissa and Jeremy went to the doctor, I was in their apartment cleaning and cooking. I was playing the song "Yet I will Praise" and singing and weeping. I went into Melissa and Jeremy's bedroom and got down on my knees to pray and beseech the Lord for my daughter's life. As I was praying, anger filled my heart. My anger was not against God, but against Satan and sin and the fall of man that created the curse on the earth. Sickness and death were not God's plan, and at this moment I felt a glimpse of God's anger, of His pain, of His sorrow. He was angry along with me for the suffering my Melissa was enduring. My God and my King hates sickness and death, but He has given the victory—He has removed the sting of death and has overcome the world (1 Corinthians 15:55-57). I went back to our house, and Mark and I waited.

Melissa called me from the car after the appointment. She said that Dr. Koonings talked to Jeremy privately, and then she said, "Mom, I've never heard anyone cry like that before."

They came right over to the house and told Mark and me that the doctor said that there were no other treatments available to help her, and that she only had weeks to months to live.

I was completely numb. I couldn't even respond. Melissa looked at me, held my hand, and said,

> " God's ways are not our ways.
> His ways are beyond finding out. "

She was a rock. She was our comfort. Again, her response stunned me. But even though she was at peace, she told us that she didn't want to die. I remember her saying, "Mom, having a husband changes everything. I want to fight for Jeremy." We were going to keep fighting—harder than ever.

Melissa had put words to an old song on the front of her medical notebook, "Is Your All on the Altar?" Her heart and commitment to God never wavered.

*"Is Your All on the Altar?"*

*You have longed for sweet peace,*
*And for faith to increase,*
*And have earnestly, fervently prayed;*
*But you cannot have rest,*
*Or be perfectly blessed,*
*Until all on the altar is laid. . . .*
*Oh, we never can know*
*What the Lord will bestow*
*Of the blessings for which we have prayed,*
*Till our body and soul*
*He doth fully control,*
*And our all on the altar is laid.*

*—"Is Your All on the Altar?" by Elisha A. Hoffman*

## *"Present your bodies a living sacrifice, holy, acceptable to God."*

*—ROMANS 12:1*

I was struggling. I remembered the angel who wept beside Melissa's hospital bed after her first surgery, and now understood her great sorrow. I thought back to the day Melissa first showed me the growth in her abdomen, and my time on the bathroom floor covering my mouth to muffle the scream so it wouldn't escape. I remembered hearing clearly from the Lord, "Here we go." The fear of that day was back again.

I know He is with me. I knew from the beginning that my Savior would travel this journey, not just close by my side but in me, filling me, strengthening me, breathing for me when I couldn't and holding me up when my legs were to weak or numb to carry me. I felt His presence, and I needed Him more now than ever. I needed to fight. I could not be weak. We were in a battle, and I needed a battle plan.

I learned quickly that if I projected ahead to my worst fear, I had no peace, no strength, only panic and anxiety. If I thought for a second, "Melissa is going to die; she only has weeks to months to live," I was worthless in the battle. The enemy could take me out with that one thought. I had to stay in the moment. If I stayed in the moment and asked God for help for today, He gave me wisdom, strength, and peace to handle what that day brought. I had to help Melissa fight her battle and leave my pain and fears in God's hands.

*God's in the heavens and does what He pleases
and is working the best for me eternally. It's not
always comfortable and convenient.*

*You can't fully understand another's pain unless you have gone through
it. May sorrow but have hope. You can comfort because you've been there
and gone through it. Must understand basic principles so when you don't
understand things going on, you fall back on what you know of the Lord.
Commit your soul as unto Him, your Creator.*

*Know the Lord has eternal purposes and plans. Never
give up what you know for what you don't! My ways
are not your ways. My ways are beyond your finding
out. The Lord doesn't owe me any explanations. Can
clay say to the potter, why have you made me such?
Or complain the process hurts? God wants to bring
the greatest value out of your life.*

*Be wholly, completely open to what God wants you to do. Don't give God limited options.*

*God knows and understands what you're going through. Praise the Lord our God who knows and loves us is taking care of us; clothing, feeding, and taking care of us. Melissa, seek first the kingdom of God and His righteousness, and all these things shall be added to you.*

*Seek first is priority #1. What God's called you to do is the Kingdom, and the other things are things. Trust God, seek God, devote yourself to God, seek first His Kingdom. You'll be mindful of heaven, and that will be your treasure. Eternity is where the focus should be. Everything else is things. Set your mind on things above. Think about sitting in the presence of the Lord forever, and all other trials and worries seem to be nothing.*

*"If then you were raised with Christ, seek those things which are above, where Christ is, sitting at the right hand of God. Set your mind on things above, not on things on the earth. For you died, and your life is hidden with Christ in God."*

—COLOSSIANS *3:1-3*

*Melissa, remember:*

> Heavenly Father, You know also if my life or death will bring You glory. I know that my life brings You glory now, and every day I'm blessed to live, I will continue to give You glory. Lord, I know You know whether more souls will come to You through my life or death. So that fear is ridiculous. Jesus, help me to fear nothing but (respectfully) You.

"Melissa—Eternity has no troubles. Eternity of blessings! So even though now you're having the wind against you, know God knows and sees what you're going through. Pray. Walk away, amazed and full of worship."

*I see my future being an awesome testimony for Your glory.*

# CHAPTER
## 11

# THE FIGHT

The news was so shocking to us that we couldn't even think of what to do. That numb feeling had taken over my mind. I can't even remember how Ryan and Megan were told or how anyone else found out the dreadful news.

We needed help. *What do we do now? How can we help Melissa?* The doctors had no plan—nothing! Others, like strong, forceful angels stepped up and began a crusade to save Melissa. People got the word out, and prayer chains for Melissa were started all over the world. KWAVE began broadcasting requests to pray for her. Others began to raise money so she could try holistic treatments, and money flowed in. Friends who loved her did research and found alternative treatments that had good results. Melissa and Jeremy decided to go to a treatment facility in Mexico. We had an army fighting! They gave us hope.

Melissa was feeling well enough to decorate a tree for Christmas. We made ornaments and had a fun evening together making her home festive before she and Jeremy left for Mexico. She loved Christmas.

Melissa and Jeremy went to the treatment center in Mexico that a friend recommended. The two of them were so in love that it was like another honeymoon. We went down to visit them. Melissa looked good, and they were really having fun together. I had made her an angel to put on the top of her tree when she got home, and she loved it.

One of the treatments Melissa was given was a coffee enema. Jeremy was insistent that he would also do it so she wouldn't be afraid. They ate the same food, including crushing large portions of fresh garlic on top of all the food they ate. There was never any complaining, just joy and trusting the Lord. I have never seen a love like theirs; I was awestruck by it. Jeremy was the best.

We were so blessed and happy that they had each other, and that our daughter had this incredible love to share.

While at the clinic, Melissa suddenly got very sick, and Jeremy had to rush her back across the border to the hospital. The alternative treatment wasn't working.

Friends stepped it up again and used their influence to get her an examination with experts at MD Anderson Cancer Center in Texas. It is supposed to be the best cancer hospital in the country. The two of them left immediately. Melissa was seen by a team of cancer specialists. Then Jeremy called me to say they were coming home. The doctors said that Melissa's cancer was surrounding her liver, and they would call her doctor and recommend a chemo regimen. It didn't sound hopeful.

On the airplane they met someone who told them about another alternate care method that recommends not to do chemotherapy, that it is really the chemo that kills you. After this conversation they had decided they were not going to do any more chemo. They decided to try a carrot juicing regiment and a strict vegan diet. I juiced carrots, made soups, and cooked some really awful-looking food. Did I really think food would cure her? I didn't know, but I was willing to try everything and anything that gave me hope of a cure. One evening I was cooking soup in Melissa's kitchen while she lay on the pullout couch in the living room. I heard her call to me, "Mom, stop cooking please! Put it outside, it smells horrible. I only want you to come and cuddle with me." In my zeal to cook the right food and juice hundreds of carrots, I was missing what was needed the most—holding her!

Melissa's chemo doctor had studied under the MD Anderson specialists Melissa had seen. They thought that a stronger chemo regimen had a chance of helping her. She needed to start immediately. Melissa's doctor agreed to the new regimen of chemo, and she decided to try. I called to set an appointment—none available. What? I drove down to the hospital, walked into his office, and demanded he see Melissa now. I wouldn't take no for an answer. I turned into one of those strong, forceful angels! She was set for a new round of chemotherapy.

Jeremy, Melissa, and I went together to see Dr. Koonings for a follow-up. I sat in the waiting room while Jeremy and Lis went in to see him. Dr. Koonings' nurse came out and sat next to me. I was just sitting quietly, reading my Bible and praying. She put her hand on my knee and said, "Are you and your daughter not close?" I was shocked.

"What? No! We are very close!" Nurse Cathy proceeded to tell me that Melissa needed her mother, and that I needed to be in the exam room with her. Jeremy was only twenty-two, and he needed help also.

Then she said, "She'll be with the angels soon." I was undone. I had been trying to let Melissa and Jeremy function as normal newlyweds, but there was nothing normal about their situation. That day I decided to be with her at every medical appointment and procedure. Jeremy and I became a team to care for Melissa and warriors fighting for her life.

Melissa became very sick about a week before Christmas. She was admitted to the hospital. We, as a family, were there constantly to provide for any need she had. As we approached Christmas Day, Melissa asked me if I would go and buy gifts that she had been thinking about for Jeremy. She also wanted me to make her favorite Christmas dishes and bring them to her hospital room on Christmas morning. Melissa's primary thought was for Jeremy. She wanted him to experience a Henning Christmas. To her, being in the hospital was not a deterrent, but an opportunity. We just had to be creative. I was determined to give her everything she asked for. Heather and I shopped and bought presents for Jeremy and all her family, just as she wanted. Heather and I became Melissa's hands and feet. We wanted to do everything she would have done and couldn't do for herself.

On Christmas Eve, Melissa was in a lot of pain. Her abdomen was swollen with fluid. I asked the nurse to please get a doctor to come and drain it. It was a procedure that Melissa had to have several times. The nurse kept telling me it was Christmas Eve and that there wasn't a doctor available. I begged her to call Dr. Koonings. She said, "No, I can't do that—it's Christmas Eve! He's with his family." It was also our Christmas Eve. We weren't gathered around a Christmas tree enjoying hot cider and cookies. We weren't smelling prime rib roasting in the oven. We weren't getting ready to go to a Christmas Eve service. We weren't hearing Christmas bells ringing or laughter that usually filled our house. Instead of being in a beautifully decorated house with all the smells and sounds of Christmas, we were in a hospital room, on the cancer floor, smelling odors and hearing sounds that I wish I could forget. This Christmas Eve our family was not gathered around a Christmas tree; instead we were gathered around Melissa's bed, praying silently and with intensity as we could see her pain increasing. I only left the room to go, again and again, to pressure the nurse to help my daughter. "Please, help her!" I know she was just doing her job, doing what she had been told. But it was unacceptable to me. Watching my child in pain was intolerable.

I'm sure it became intolerable for the nurse as well, or possibly I became intolerable to her, I don't know. She never hinted to me that she had made the call, but it became obvious that she had when Dr. Koonings walked in. He left his family's Christmas Eve dinner to come and care for Melissa. We were so thankful. He was gracious and kind and showed an obvious love for Melissa. She was easy to love, and they seemed to have a special relationship. He spent many hours with her on several occasions, draining bottles of fluid from her abdomen. They would talk like friends. Melissa was always asking him how he was and was genuinely interested in his life and his family. Dr. Koonings was the best Christmas gift. He relieved her pain, and she was able to sleep in peace.

In all the stress of caring for Melissa, I had not been paying attention to Megan. She came over and sat next to me. She told me she wasn't feeling well, and that she had a stomachache. I was really upset at her for being there when she thought she was sick. It would be detrimental to Melissa if she caught something. I told her to go home and asked Heather to take her. Heather later called and told me Megan had thrown up several times out the car window on the way home. I had to get home to do all the Christmas meal cooking that Melissa wanted anyway, so I left the hospital for home. I went into Megan's room to see her, and she was in bed with what we assumed was the stomach flu. I was upset—I remember being terrible to her. I had no compassion, as though all my compassion was used up on Melissa and I had none left to give. The exhaustion and emotional stress of the day had taken their toll.

Megan is my youngest. She was always strong and covered her emotions well. I loved her personality; she could always make us laugh. She could get her siblings to do anything for her and quickly learned to bypass Mom to get what she wanted. She was very independent and rarely needed me. This night she needed me, and I failed her. It is one of my lowest moments and biggest regrets. I have four children, but my total focus was on the weakest, the one in the most danger. Meanwhile, Megan was in danger and I couldn't see it.

I cooked throughout the night to prepare the meal Melissa had asked for, her favorite: chicken and dumplings! She also wanted what we ate every Christmas—sweet potato casserole with pecan topping, green bean casserole, and our most loved Christmas tradition, cinnamon rolls and sticky buns. As I cooked, I would check on Megan occasionally. She was sick all night. In the morning I asked Mark to check on her, and he found her in a great deal of pain. Now I became concerned. I checked her out and knew she needed to go to the hospital. Mark rushed her down to the hospital where Melissa was while I packed up the food. I dropped the food off in Melissa's room and immediately went to the emergency room to see what was happening with Megan. She had appendicitis and needed surgery immediately.

It was Christmas morning, and two of my babies were in the hospital, one gravely ill and the other in surgery. One on the third floor and the other on the second floor. I would go back and forth, up and down the stairs throughout the day checking on both of them, all the while trying to give Melissa the Christmas dinner she so wanted to share with Jeremy.

Megan was out of surgery but was not waking up from the anesthesia. The nurses were concerned. She should have been in and out of surgery and been able to go home a couple of hours later. Now they were saying they are going to have to admit her. She just would not wake up! I was now by my youngest child's bedside, praying and asking God to spare her life and wake her up. As they prepared to admit her, I asked if they could put her on the same wing as Melissa. "No, that is a cancer ward. She will need to be on the general surgery floor." Heather took over when I had no strength left and kept advocating for them to put Megan on the same floor as Melissa. I think they had mercy on me and pulled some strings and got approval to put Megan in an available room right next to Melissa. We could have Christmas together.

We opened presents around Melissa's bed with Jeremy, Mark, Heather, and me. Melissa was still very weak but also so happy. I had bought Melissa some J'Adore perfume that she loved. She had spent lots of time choosing the perfect scent for her wedding, and this was it! We both loved it. She opened her present as I was opening mine from her—she had Heather buy me the exact same perfume. Melissa and I loved that little God moment; it was so sweet. Megan did finally wake up, and we rolled her bed into Melissa's room so they could be together. It was not the typical family Christmas. Heather said, "People are going to feel really sorry for us." Maybe, but I was thankful for so much. Dr. Koonings caring enough to give up his Christmas Eve to relieve Melissa's pain, forgiveness that is available through Jesus and that Megan freely gave to me, Mark being such a good husband and father, Jeremy's love and attentiveness to Melissa, Megan waking up, Heather's persistence, nurses who went the extra mile, a room available next to Melissa, J'Adore perfume, and especially the love we all had for each other.

> "Every moment together is a gift, no matter the circumstances or surroundings."

Melissa had Jeremy and her family. She was happy.

The next morning, both Melissa and Megan were feeling better. Megan was able to stay in Melissa's room and hang out there with her IV. They took a walk around the ward together holding the teddy bears I had bought them. Every Christmas since the girls were little, I had bought them matching teddy bears, and this year was no exception. That afternoon Megan was strong enough to go home, and Melissa followed the next day.

On the day of her discharge, a social worker at the hospital came into Melissa's room. She asked Melissa if she had any questions or if she could help in any way. Yes, Melissa had a question, something that bothered her, and she needed an answer. Melissa struggled with eating disorders in her teens, and she had convinced herself that it had caused her to get cancer. So she asked, "Did I do this to myself because of my eating disorder?" The social worker talked to her for a while, trying to convince her that eating disorders had nothing to do with ovarian cancer.

Melissa still wondered about it. She wanted to tell her story about eating disorders to encourage other young women take better care of themselves.

She wrote about her struggle with her self-image, striving for perfection, and focusing on food. Melissa was an open book now and desired to share her life—good and bad—with others. Her hope was that God would use her to help them walk in freedom and the acceptance of her Savior Jesus Christ.

Before Melissa left the hospital, she wanted to write thank-you notes to the nurses. She sat on her bed for a long time working on them. She wasn't in a hurry to leave. The nurses were important to her, and she wanted each of them to know how much she appreciated them and that they were precious to her and to God. She wasn't going to leave until she wrote each nurse a separate personal note.

# CHAPTER
## 12

# HOME

*"Not knowing the things that will happen to me there, except that the Holy Spirit testifies in every city, saying that chains and tribulations await me. But none of these things move me; nor do I count my life dear to myself, so that I may finish my race with joy, and the ministry which I received from the Lord Jesus, to testify to the gospel of the grace of God."*

ACTS 20:22-24 (MY POWER VERSE)

Melissa's care became more intense. She had a home health nurse come and set up IVs and provide syringes. Jeremy was so great with giving Lis her medications, shots, and keeping the IV machine working. We had essential oils that we would rub on her feet and natural serum to help her with her appetite. Jeremy never complained and served Melissa with joy.

One day Lis was feeling very sick and was cuddled up on the pullout couch in their living room. She really liked that because she could see me cooking and she could look outside onto their balcony. She just loved her apartment and the way she and Jeremy had decorated it. Someone had given them the name of Jesus to hang on the wall. It was exactly like the metal piece that hung in the church they were married in. Megan came over and crawled into bed with her. She put her face next to Melissa's face, nose-to-nose, and sang through her tears the entire song "My Father's Eyes." It was so beautiful. I thought she was going to stop singing because she was crying, but she sang every word to every verse of the song they both loved so much. It was the song they would sing to each other as they would go to bed at night. Melissa gently stroked Megan's face as tears flowed from all three of us cuddling in her bed.

Melissa and Jeremy had decided to try another chemo regimen. I drove Melissa down to Zion hospital for her treatment. This chemo treatment was different than before. The nurse needed to put in a PICC line, a thin, flexible tube that had to be inserted into a vein in her arm then threaded into a large vein above her heart. I about fainted just hearing what she had to do. But it was the best way to give her chemotherapy, and it would stay in place so she wouldn't have to have repeated needle sticks. I could see the pain on Melissa's face during the procedure. I quoted Philippians 3:10:

*"that I may know Him and the power of His resurrection, and the fellowship of His sufferings . . ."*

I stopped before the last phrase—

*"being conformed to His death."*

"Melissa, this is part of your fellowship of His suffering."

She was quick to say, "Oh no, Mom, this is nothing compared to what Jesus went through for me."

She continued to stun and amaze me. Not once did I ever hear Melissa complain about any procedure or the ghastly medicines she had to swallow or the shots she had to take. She definitely cried out in pain many times. Occasionally she would say, "Cancer hurts." But there was no self-pity.

The drip, drip of chemo began once again. The first round of chemo Melissa looked and felt healthy and was all about ministering to her fellow cancer patients. This time she looked and felt sick. I wouldn't leave her, and she didn't want me to. The nurse would check on her periodically. At the end she checked her heart rate, and it was up to 145 beats a minute. The nurse called Melissa's oncologist, and he said, "I told her to go into hospice; there is nothing we can do." The doctor Melissa loved and trusted had changed. It seemed to me like he had given up. I was scared, and I felt completely helpless. The nurse said I could take her to the emergency room, where they would have to help her. I asked Melissa what she wanted to do.

"I want to go home."

I called Jeremy and asked him to call people to pray. Her heart rate was too fast. The nurse made it sound like she could die at any moment. I prayed, "Please, Lord, don't let her die in the car. Don't let her die without Jeremy and her family with her. Please." As we drove home, Melissa lay in the back seat and I reached back and held her hand and sang to her. I knew she needed to worship, and she needed my touch. I sang a song that she loved.

> So close I believe You're holding me now. In Your hands I belong, You'll never let me go . . .

She would comment, "So beautiful, Mom." We loved to worship. We felt His presence and knew He was holding us both and that He would never let go!

When I pulled into the parking lot of their apartment, I noticed an unusual number of cars. I ran up to get Jeremy so he could carry Melissa upstairs. Their apartment was full of people. Jeremy had called people to pray, and they all decided to come over and pray. That was not what I had in mind! Jeremy got Melissa into bed. Someone had decided to do a healing ceremony. Melissa had many of these, but we still believed they were powerful. I had studied the Scriptures a lot, and it was really important to me that we did exactly what the Scriptures said:

*"Is anyone among you suffering? Let him pray. Is anyone cheerful? Let him sing psalms. Is anyone among you sick? Let him call for the elders of the church, and let them pray over him, anointing him with oil in the name of the Lord. And the prayer of faith will save the sick, and the Lord will raise him up. And if he has committed sins, he will be forgiven. Confess your trespasses to one another and pray for one another, that you may be healed. The effective, fervent prayer of a righteous man avails much. Elijah was a man with a nature like ours, and he prayed earnestly that it would*

*not rain; and it did not rain on the land for three years and six months. And he prayed again, and the heaven gave rain, and the earth produced its fruit."*

—*James 5:13-18*

Many of the healing ceremonies Melissa had were not done according to these instructions. Mark and I had many discussions about healing in the Bible. We knew Jesus healed and that He still could heal. We knew that He miraculously removed a tumor from her body after one humble man joined in praying with Jeremy and Melissa. There were many others who came and prayed prayers for healing over her, and each one was greatly appreciated. Mark had a difficult time, especially when people would command or claim her healing as if their will would be done by the commanding words they spoke. I kept coming back to studying James 5 and wanted to see this followed exactly as written. Mark had been in the ministry for years and had participated in many anointings for healing. Now it was his daughter. What exactly were God's instructions to those who were to pray over the sick? It says the sick should call upon the elders of the church. They are to pray over them, anoint them with oil in the name of the Lord, and their prayer of faith will save the sick.

This Scripture was burning in my mind as I saw a room full of young, well intentioned men and women. I knew they loved my daughter, but they were not the "elders of the church." Jeremy was waiting for Joey Buran, a pastor at Calvary Chapel Costa Mesa, and Bill Welsh, senior pastor at Calvary Chapel Huntington Beach. When they arrived, the crowd got up to move into Melissa's room. I spoke up and asked Joey if they could follow James 5 exactly and please could the others stay out and pray in the living room with me. The women were kind enough to stay with me and pray.

There was a lot of confidence and declarations of her healing. As her heart rate went down into the 120s, faith and confidence grew. I went in to see how my sweet girl was doing. The guests in her home were on her mind. Melissa asked me to serve everyone cookies and get them something to drink. Again, I became her hands and feet, doing what she would do if she could—serving others. She had baked white chocolate macadamia nut cookies the day before, and hoped there was enough for everyone. I focused on her guests, but really all I wanted was for everyone to go home. I was serving all these people while my sick daughter was in the bedroom by herself. I was making sure everyone was getting a cookie and something to drink. It seemed like a party atmosphere to me. Jeremy was enjoying his friends and there was lots of laughing and loud talking. In my mind I was screaming, "My daughter could be dying, and you all are having a party?" I went into Melissa's room and saw her crying. "Oh, Mom, I was just praying and asking the Lord to send you or Jeremy to me." I climbed in bed, held her, and tickled her back. I stayed with her until the people left and Jeremy came in to take over snuggling and comforting her.

Melissa would rebound, and we would all have hope.

Yes, Melissa was feeling stronger, but she was not "healed." The prayers of faith did not save her, nor did the Lord raise her up. At least not in the way we thought. I continued to ponder James 5. I thought about the other times that pastors had come and prayed and anointed her with oil. Some were hesitant to pray for healing. Some would read Psalm 23 or other Scripture to her. One gave her a mustard seed and reminded her that the faith of a mustard seed could move mountains. She loved it. She genuinely loved and appreciated every pastor and friend who came to visit and pray for her.

As I studied James 5 again, it became clear to me that it was more about the elders who came to pray than it was about the sick person. Often we take a verse out of context and fail to see the big picture or the entire instruction. It is the elder's prayer of faith that God uses to heal, not the faith of the sick. Too many sick people have been made to feel that their faith isn't strong enough; that they aren't healed because of their little faith. I love that God dispels that in this text. Melissa's faith was strong, and God was moving mountains in her life. It just wasn't visible to us.

"Confess your trespasses to one another, and pray for one another, that you may be healed. The effective, fervent prayer of a righteous man avails much."

—JAMES 5:16

> Melissa, count it all joy while going through this trial, knowing the testing of your faith produces patience. And let it have its perfect work, so you'll be perfect (mature) and complete, lacking nothing.

Melissa began to become frailer and sicker. It was so difficult for Ryan to see his beloved little sister suffering and wasting away. He could hardly speak. Oh, how she loved her brother! Lis would reach out her arms to him, and he would bend his tall body down to her face, then her little arms would reach around his neck and hold him as tight as she could. Jean-Luc Lajoie also came over to the apartment to see her. Melissa loved worship, so Jean-Luc began to play and sing. We all praised God together, and even in Melissa's weakness, she raised her arms as high as she could, as was her habit while praising the Lord. We gave Melissa a pedicure and massaged her feet. We all adored her so much. Jean-Luc began to sing a song He wrote for her, "Melissa." It was beautiful. She was lifted into her Savior's presence in worship, and the peace of the Lord shone on her face.

# CHAPTER

## 13

## HEAVEN

> "The body I am in is only a house
> that the words of my mouth
> that come from my heart dwell in."

*E*ven though my eyes have not seen You, I feel You. Even though I have not met You face-to-face, I know You. You are in my heart and in my life. You are the King whom I ask to sit on the throne of my life. How beautiful You have made this earth. I look up to the blue sky, and I am in awe of Your splendor. You are so amazing. Lord, I want to praise You morning, noon, and night. How my heart has changed! I long to be in heaven. My soul earnestly desires to be in Your Kingdom. I was going to say presence, yet I am already there.

*These bodies are not meant for eternal life. These temporal bodies are just that— temporal. They are subject to the effects of the curse on the earth. These bodies are decaying, and we groan longing for our eternal bodies. Jesus is the healer. He has healed all our diseases in the eternal state with glorified bodies that will never suffer decay!*

*—2 Corinthians 5:1-2*

Dr. Koonings' nurse Cathy became very special to Melissa. Cathy invited Melissa and Jeremy over for dinner, and Lis was so excited. She had planned to make lasagna and take it over. The next morning, she had an appointment with Dr. Koonings to remove fluid in her abdomen. But that night Melissa became very sick and was in tremendous pain. She was so sad she couldn't go to the dinner. Jeremy and I rushed her to the hospital emergency room. The emergency doctor was wonderful and helped stabilize Melissa and got her pain under control. He told me that if she had the fluid removed, she would die immediately. Her fluid levels and enzymes were completely out of control. Jeremy was so exhausted, he went and slept in the car. I waited by Melissa's bedside all night sitting in a chair, bent over with my head on her bed. In the morning Dr. Koonings arrived to see her. He came to remove her fluid and told me she could die today. I answered, "No! She is not going to die today!" She needed her family to be with her. I discussed with him what the emergency room doctor had said about her fluid levels. I insisted that he cautiously only remove enough fluid to ease her pain. He was unhappy with me but complied. Her chemo doctor then came to see her and discussed with her a DNR (Do not resuscitate order). She understood exactly what he was saying, and she specifically told him that she did not want that and would not sign a DNR. She was still fighting for her life and expected them to fight with her.

The doctor finally decided to move her to a room on the third floor. As I was leaving the emergency room, several nurses came over to me and hugged me with tears in their eyes, saying, "I'm so sorry." I couldn't respond.

After Melissa was settled, Jeremy noticed that she had no IV fluids and no monitors had been put on her. Then I noticed there was a DNR sign on the door. We called the nurse, and she confirmed there was a DNR for Melissa. They were not going to give her IV fluids to keep her hydrated and comfortable. They were not going to monitor her. They were giving up. We asked to see the doctor immediately. We had some intense talks to get them to honor Melissa's wishes. This became on ongoing conversation with doctors and nurses.

The Bible Says,

> *"One day is as a thousand years,*
> *and a thousand years as one day".*
>
> —2 PETER 3:8

One day of life can have an impact for a thousand years! That is how Melissa felt, and she knew she was to continue her fight. Her life was not over yet.

After Jeremy, Mark, and I had a very heated conversation with the doctor, he removed the DNR sign from her door and from her chart. They began IV fluids and started monitoring her as she deserved. The doctor had concerns that the IV fluids would exacerbate her ascites, which is the fluid buildup in the abdomen that causes so much pain. But an amazing thing happened. Because Dr. Koonings did not remove all the fluid in the morning, the needle hole in her abdomen did not close up as it usually did. Fluid slowly seeped and never filled up her abdomen again.

Jeremy's family joined us at the hospital. Melissa was sound asleep and gravely ill, but not one of us believed she was near death. We were continually beseeching the Lord for His mercy and praying the Word over her as we circled her bed. Lis woke crying, and I instinctively as a mother began to soothe her, saying, "Don't cry, honey." She looked at me and said, "No, it's okay to cry—it is so beautiful." She had tears of joy, fulfillment, and awe in the sweet aroma of prayers ascending to her Lord. Melissa and I had this in common, that we would weep when we were touched by the Spirit. It was so beautiful to her to hear her family who raised her to walk and love Jesus united with her new family that God so graciously gave her. Love and unity—Jesus prayed that for His body, and how beautiful it is to behold.

The next two weeks were precious. There were good days and bad days. There were days when she felt well enough to have friends over for pizza and share their love story like newlyweds do. Days of friends and family coming to see her and share their love with her. Days for loving Jeremy and loving her family. Jeremy and I both slept in her room every night. One morning Jeremy woke up and asked Melissa how she was feeling. "Great!" she said. With excitement, he responded, "I dreamed you would say 'great!'"

Remember the friends who were like strong, forceful angels stepping up and crusading to save Melissa's life? One of those angels was Cathy Geier. Melissa had worked for her as a nanny to her children. Melissa loved the Geier family, and they loved her. Cathy continued to talk to medical experts and find treatments that might help Lis survive, things like blood transfusions that improved her strength and gave her a "great" day or another chemo drug that sounded promising that her doctor agreed to. Everyone was still fighting hard. Melissa had faith to believe God would heal her, and she shared with me her desire to throw a big party to say thank you to all the people who helped her. She especially wanted to bless Cathy. She loved concocting different drinks with juices and sodas at the hospital. She was formulating a recipe to share with all those who came to her "thank you" party.

One night when she was very sick, with family and friends around her hospital bed, a pastor came in to pray. He began his prayer by telling the Lord that we were all tired. He was giving God permission to take Melissa home right then because we were TIRED! Melissa had asked me over the course of her illness, "Why do people come to pray if they are not going to pray for healing?" Oh, how she loved coming boldly into the throne room of heaven and asking for the impossible, because she believed all things are possible with God. Matthew 19:26 says, "But Jesus looked at them and said to them, 'With men this is impossible, but with God all things are possible.'"

Similarly, Hebrews 4:16 says,

*"Let us therefore come boldly to the throne of grace, that we may obtain mercy and find grace to help in time of need."*

> Lord, as Your child I run to take my rightful seat.

How amazing is that? Melissa described prayer as running to take her rightful seat in her Father's throne room, where she could boldly ask for anything. I imagine her running and jumping on to her Father's lap, where He engulfs her in His arms and listens to her every word. She longed for pastors and Christians to pray like that and to beseech the God of heaven for her healing. She was ready for heaven, but she was still fighting for Jeremy. She just couldn't give up for him. She would fight and endure until there was no breath left. It was the promise she made in her heart when she decided to tell him she loved him. She had to give it her all.

In those two weeks, I never left the hospital. I was there to serve Melissa and Jeremy and to fight for her and what she wanted and needed. We played worship music constantly in her room. Jeremy would sing to her and write songs. I would pray and read the Word to her. We would talk and we would listen. Nurse Cathy would come and see her. Mark had met with her outside of Melissa's room and led her to the Lord, an answer to Melissa's prayers. Cathy went into the room and laid on top of Melissa and gave her a huge hug. She cried and told her Jesus was now in her heart. One day can impact not just a thousand years, but eternity!

One day Mark went in to have some alone time with his daughter. He cherished her. She was not just his daughter, she was one of his disciples. She had a heart for evangelism just like her dad. She loved Thursday night Bible Study, where she could listen to her dad teach the Bible. She would often write him cute notes about how much she loved and appreciated him. On this day, she gave him some advice that he has cherished and shares often with others: "Dad, many people come to visit me in the hospital, and they are worried and troubled by so many things. But those things don't matter. Here is what I have learned through all of this . . .

life is a gift, and it is to be fully appreciated."

Oh, yes. Each day of life is a gift. Use it to love well and make a difference in people's lives for eternity.

The nurses and doctors on call who did not know Melissa would come and give the DNR talk again and again, the quality of life talks, as if they knew the quality of her life and what each breath meant to her. These doctors were horrible—they decided what they thought was best and would continue to come into the room to pressure Jeremy for a DNR. Everyone had an opinion, and the decision was tearing Jeremy apart. I said, "Jeremy, go and ask Melissa." It was her decision to make without any pressure from anyone. Jeremy went into her room by himself to talk to his precious wife and ask her what she wanted to do. She decided. Jeremy came out crying and told the doctor she decided the DNR was OK. I went in to talk with her. "Jesus will be your life support, honey." She nodded and smiled with the peace of God.

The family all stayed the night at the hospital. On February 4th I woke up and decided we were going to open the curtains, bring in the light, and praise God today. It would be a glorious day. Something was different about today. Melissa had been heavily sedated because of her pain and hadn't been awake for a long time. The family all came into her room, and then more people began to arrive. The room was now crowded. I never could understand why people thought they should be there under these circumstances.

I asked Jeremy's mother to sing "Heaven Is a Wonderful Place" with me. We each got on one side of the bed and began to sing about heaven. Melissa woke up and looked at me and said in a very strong voice, "NO, NO! Jeremy, it's all gone away. Jeremy, you have to believe me, it's all gone away."

He came close to her and said, "Are you healed?"

She shouted, "Yes! Yes!" She then got out of bed and walked toward the bathroom. A nurse came in and told her to get back in bed. I told her Melissa could do whatever she wanted! She did get back in bed, and immediately fell asleep. I noticed that her stomach was not swollen as before, and I couldn't see any of the tumors through her skin anymore.

I believe, Lord help my unbelief!

A family member had said earlier, "God is going to do a miracle, and I am here to see it! I am not leaving—I don't want to miss the miracle."

Some in Jesus day stayed with Jesus watching for the miracles; waiting to see signs and wonders. They were enthralled with the show. Some, as Mary, were there to love Him and to serve Him. I could see the same contrasting priorities in many of the people who had crowded the room that day. The interesting thing was that when God chose to show us a glimpse of His strength and healing power, the person who most longed to see it, missed it. They were not in the room to see God raise Melissa out of her bed and to hear her declare her healing!

I felt many had crowded into Melissa's room that day hoping to see a miracle. They were always looking and seeking for the miracle report, even to the point of making things sound better than what they were. God did not need any help; He does not need anyone exaggerating His miracles.

There was a lot of excitement. The crowd of people left. One pastor rushed out to call KWAVE, and they announced on the radio that Melissa had been healed. It was a beautiful gift when they all left to finally be alone with Melissa. Jeremy was so excited and believed with all his heart that his beautiful wife was healed. God had answered their prayers in a spectacular way, just as He had done before. It was easy to believe; we had seen His miraculous power before. Jeremy was insistent that the doctors stop her pain meds, and he wanted a sonogram to prove she was healed. He was convinced God had healed her. I was concerned about lowering her pain medication because I had seen the horrifying results of breakthrough pain, and I didn't want my daughter suffering. He told me that God would not dangle a carrot in front of his face and then yank it away. His faith was strong and undeniable, and it strengthened mine. I believed.

Jeremy did convince the doctor to reduce her pain meds. Heather was cradling Melissa and telling Jeremy no. He would not listen. Jeremy was exhausted physically and emotionally. He went to take a nap, finally able to sleep in peace. Melissa also slept for hours. I stayed by her side. All of her friends, along with Megan and Ryan, went to church. It was Sunday night and they all had the habit of going to The Rock. They were excited and convinced of Melissa's healing, so they felt comfortable leaving the hospital.

After the reduction in pain medication, Melissa began to wake up and was struggling to breathe. Respiratory therapists were called to suction her airway. Heather never left her side. Mark joined her. They both were the strongest in the family, Heather at her side and Mark at the foot of her bed. It was excruciating to watch my daughter struggle to breathe. There isn't a strong enough word to describe the horror I felt as I watched the panic on her face as she gasped for air. I began to pace back and forth, praying and walking the circular cancer ward as the respiratory therapists worked on her. As I walked the halls of the cancer floor, I felt Satan walking beside me, smiling. He thinks this is his domain. He revels in the suffering of others, especially God's children. I felt the grief of the Holy Spirit and the anger of God against him and the original sin that brought about this terrible suffering. I prayed against the devil—against the evil and for miracles of healing as I passed every room. I declared that Jesus is victorious. He who is in me is greater than He who is in the world. And I felt Satan's presence depart.

God's miracle of healing was to come in a different way than what I wanted. Melissa continued to struggle to breathe. Mark and I asked the doctor to please help her, please increase her medication so she would not be suffering. He did, and she was able to fall back to sleep and be at peace.

Tears rolled softly down Melissa's face. They devastated Jeremy and were breaking my heart. She looked so disappointed to me, and maybe she was. She believed in her healing as much as Jeremy did. But as I looked at her face with her big eyes and huge tears streaming down her cheeks, I remembered her words to me from just a week before as I told her not to cry. "No, it's okay to cry—it is so beautiful." I believe her tears were brought on by the touch of the Spirit giving her a glimpse of heaven and "It was so beautiful!"

Jeremy went into a private room across the hall with his parents. He was understandably shaken and not doing well. Heather and I sat on each side of Melissa into the late night of February 4. Just after midnight on February 5, her breathing began to slow. Megan and Ryan had come back from church, but Megan was not in the room or hallway, and I had to find her. I knew Melissa wanted all of her family with her, so I jumped up and ran downstairs to find her and then rushed back. When we walked back up, the hall was filled with Melissa's friends. They were quietly sitting on the floor with their backs to the wall, keeping a distance from the room. They looked like angels to me, filling the hallways waiting for Melissa to join them.

I told Megan, "When Melissa takes her last breath, I will take mine!"

"No, Mom, she is not dying!" We walked into Melissa's room just as she took her last breath. Heather had her arm around Melissa and was saying over and over again, "I love you; I love you; I love you." I quickly came to the other side of Melissa and joined in saying, "I love you; I love you; I love you" as we wept. Megan screamed and ran out of the room. Ryan fell to the floor in a fetal position and wept. John Leeder, a pastor who had walked this journey with us, came in and engulfed Ryan on the floor with his huge arms and wept along with us.

Jeremy came into the room with his parents, and I moved aside to let him be near her. I just kept weeping and saying to him, "I'm sorry, I'm sorry." I was brokenhearted for my loss and equally, painfully, brokenhearted for Jeremy. Heather then walked over to the CD player and hit play. "Yet I Will Praise" is a song that we sang often together. It is a song that Melissa and Jeremy clung to and would weep with. It is her heart, and it is ours. We sang and we lifted our hands to heaven as Melissa so often did. Jeremy tried to raise his arms, but he couldn't; he was too weak. His father got behind him and lifted his arms for him and held them up as we all praised the Lord our God in our darkest valley, when our world was shattered and all hope was gone.

*I will praise You Lord my God*
*Even in my brokenness*
*I will praise You Lord*
*I will praise You Lord my God*
*Even in my desperation*
*I will praise You Lord*

*And I can't understand*
*All that You allow*
*I just can't see the reason*
*But my life is in Your hands*
*and though I cannot see You*
*I choose to trust You*

*Even when my heart is torn*
*I will praise You Lord*
*Even when I feel deserted*
*I will praise You Lord*
*Even in the darkest valley*
*I will praise You Lord*
*And when my world is shattered*
*And it seems all hope is gone*
*Yet I will praise You Lord*

*I will trust You Lord my God,*
*Even in my loneliness*
*I will trust You Lord*
*I will trust You Lord my God,*
*Even when I cannot hear you*
*I will trust You Lord*

*And I will not forget*
*That You hung on a cross*
*Lord You bled and died for me*
*And if I have to suffer*
*I know that You've been there*
*And I know that You're here now*

"YET I WILL PRAISE" WRITTEN BY ANDY PARK

It was over. It felt like all our hope was gone and we were shattered. Slowly the hope of heaven filled my heart. My faith became stronger.

*"Jesus said to her, 'I am the resurrection and the life. He who believes in Me, though he may die, he shall live. And whoever lives and believes in Me shall never die. Do you believe this?' She said to Him, 'Yes, Lord, I believe that You are the Christ, the Son of God, who is to come into the world.'"*

—*JOHN 11:25-27*

Yes, Lord, I believe! Melissa believes. Melissa was exactly where she wanted to be—with Jesus, her Savior, face-to-face, safely home. This is what our faith is all about.

Jeremy was lying on the hospital floor in the fetal position, just bawling. A nurse came into the room and went over to Melissa and kept calling out her name. "Melissa! Mrs. Camp! Melissa!"

What is he doing? Did he expect her to just wake up? It was unsettling, to say the least.

I went out into the hall and stood next to Jeremy's dad. He had called his church and told them the news. They had been praying for a mighty miracle along with us. He had just gotten a call, and I heard him say, "No, the Lord has spoken. He has made His will clear." He shared with me that the caller was asking if they were to expect God to resurrect her. Faith ran deep for so many. They were invested in Melissa and Jeremy's lives and had prayed fervently and earnestly for them.

I had learned through this journey that we pray for healing just like Melissa had said. We run to take our rightful seat, and we pray BIG impossible prayers because we have a God who hears, and we have a God who does the impossible. We pray like that until God's will is finally revealed. Her resurrection will come, but not today.

# CHAPTER
## 14

# COMFORT

*I* am all alone. It is so dark. Where is everyone? What am I doing? Where am I? The parking lot—oh yes, I need to find my car . . . what car? I can't remember what car I have. Where is it? What lot did I park it in? I'm walking, but I can't feel my feet hit the ground. Why can't I feel the ground? My arms are so heavy. They must weigh 100 pounds each. I can't lift them. Why can't I feel my feet hitting the ground? Where am I? Oh yes, the car. I'm lost; I'm alone; I can't feel my body. Jesus, help me! It's so dark. I can't see. What do I do, where do I go? Why can't I feel my feet hitting the ground? Jesus? "Look up, Janette." My head is completely numb; I can't feel it; it is too heavy; I can't lift it. "Look up, Janette." Ryan—he's so far away. I see him driving his truck. He's too far away. Lord, he won't see me. He's coming, he's coming to get me. My son.

Grief does strange things to you. I was numb, confused, and couldn't remember simple things. I don't remember leaving the hospital. I don't know where my family was or why I was alone. Why was I alone? Later, as I was pondering this, I could hear Melissa's voice say to me, "Jesus and I were with you, Mom." I believe that.

I was wandering down a very dark road between two parking lots when I heard, "Look up, Janette" and there was Ryan exiting the far parking lot. I thought it was supernatural that he could even see me; it was so dark. He did come and pick me up. He found a friend to find my car and drive it home for me.

As we found our way home on that black night, I kept thinking I could never pray again. How could I ask God for anything again? Everything seemed trivial. I was without strength, completely empty, and couldn't pray.

I finally fell asleep, and when I awoke, I found myself praising my Lord and Savior. I could not ask Him for anything, but I also could not breathe without Him. Praises were continually in my heart towards my Savior who prepared a place in heaven for my daughter and one day would take me to her. I was grateful. That morning the Holy Spirit took over my heart and mind and formulated a love language between Jesus my Savior and me. He truly is close to the brokenhearted and comforts those who mourn. I didn't need to ask Him for anything. He knew what I needed, and He was there to hold on to me just as I told Melissa He would do for her. I longed to know everything about heaven. I began to read and study everything I could, and my God comforted me. His comfort and strength were unexplainable. His peace was beautiful.

*"Let not your heart be troubled; you believe in God, believe also in Me. In My Father's house are many mansions; if it were not so, I would have told you. I go to prepare a place for you. And if I go and prepare a place for you, I will come again and receive you to Myself; that where I am, there you may be also."*

—JOHN 14:1-3

Jeremy and his family rushed off to Indiana the day after Melissa's memorial service, four days after she had died. Mark called Jeremy and left messages, but in his grief, numbness, and confusion he could not talk. My thought had been that we would "comfort one another." Why were we all so unable to do that?

We were all ill prepared for the intense sorrow that comes from the death of a deeply loved wife, daughter, sister, daughter-in-law, and friend. In Philippians 2:27, Paul refers to this grief as "sorrow upon sorrow." It hit hard! Each one of us, Hennings and Camps, had to find our comfort in our own way. The only comfort I remember was from Jesus. My Jesus, my strength, my joy, my comfort, my love, my life.

There was one thing that continued to bother me. I never asked God why He took my precious Melissa home so soon. I knew the answer: He loved her. All His ways are good and kind. He had a plan, and it was still being played out. That's all I needed to know. But there was one thing that I finally asked Him about. I did not understand why He had her wake up and declare she was healed the day before she died. It devastated Jeremy and confused so many. I simply asked the Lord, "What was that all about?"

I sweetly heard His answer: "I wanted you all to know that I heard your prayers. I saw your fasting and your faith. I wanted you to know that I did heal her, but it was My will to take Melissa to heaven on February 5, 2001." It had always been His will, and I believe Melissa was healed as she had said:

> Whether You heal me now, later, or in heaven, it's all good to me.

It was all good with me as well, and I knew He would carry me through my darkest times, just as He did for Melissa. *I'm so glad I have Your love and peace to bring me through this.*

Before Melissa's wedding, she took me aside and said, "Mom, I have something I want you to keep for me. They're my journals, and I want you to have them." Now I found the box, picked out a journal, and began reading.

*I thank You for my parents. O Lord, You gave me the greatest parents in all the earth. I truly believe that when You had me in thought, You searched the world for my special parents. Lord Jesus, I praise Your name for giving me to them, and in return, them to me. Thank You that my father raised us in the way we should go. Thank You for his light for the world shining into my eyes, his passion for ministry and the unsaved being passed onto me. I thank You for the wonderful father he has been and continues to be. I thank You for him being so forgiving to me. I know I do not deserve it, or anything. He is a wonderful Father. Thank You for teaching him how to be. Thank You for restoring our relationship, may it grow further to overflowing.*

*Oh Lord, my mother, how can I begin to express the thanks owed to You? You have blessed me with a mother everyone dreams of, and yet at times, I have taken her for granted. Thank You for my precious Mom. Lord, she is a godly woman. She has taught me so much, and continues to do so daily. You have taught me so much by my mother, thank You. Lord, I love her immensely. Tears pour down my face at the thought of separation from her, but I know that we will be spending eternity together. Lord, if You were, for some reason, to take my life sooner than we all had planned, I pray You would comfort my Mom. I know as much as I have needed her, she has needed me. Her heart has given so much love to me, so many memories, laughter, talks, fellowship, advice, counsel, friendship, and so much more. My mother has been my best friend. What other seventeen-year-old can say that? Lord, You have blessed my youth by my family. If my parents were an ounce different, I would be also. I thank You for them. I thank You so much.*

*I remember when I first went to Hawaii, and on the plane ride home, how I longed to see my Dad, to hold his hand, to love him. That feeling has returned. I pray that daily I will long to love my father. I pray that daily I may long to love my family—my mother, brother, sisters, grandmas, grandpa, uncles, aunts, cousins and brothers and sisters in Christ, and all those lost lambs. I pray that my number one love will not be for my parents or family, friends, or a possession, but it will be You, my Jesus, my Lord, my God, my love, my life.*

> "The true reason I live is to glorify You. Help me to be used so You can reach the lost. I love You, Jesus; see You soon."

As I read those words, tears poured down my face. At the age of seventeen, Melissa was praying for God to comfort me if she were to die. God our Father was now using her own words to do just that. I began to spend hours reading through her journals, and Melissa's prayer was answered—I was comforted! But even more than that, I was transformed. The intimacy of her walk with God challenged me and grew me in my faith and my relationship with Jesus. I was learning from my daughter how to handle this difficult broken road that I was now traveling. She counseled me as if she were sitting right next to me. Her words catapulted me out of depression, anguish, and grief into the presence of the King, where I found the trials and worries of this life faded away and were replaced with peace and fullness of His joy.

> "Learn from sorrow, seek God, be hungry for Him, and you'll be happy."

God was also using Melissa's journals to show me His faithful plans for her life and that He had answered her prayers and given her the desires of her heart.

*"'For I know the plans that I have for you,' declares the LORD, 'plans for welfare and not for calamity to give you a future and a hope.'"*

—*JEREMIAH 29:11, NASB*

His plans for Melissa were and are amazing! Just like she said, "Oh, Mom! That is so great, God is going to do such amazing things!" Yes, He did, and He is still is.

God's amazing plan included Jeremy Camp. I grieve that he had to experience such horrific pain and sorrow, but I have joy in the fruit of it. By faith, Jeremy picked up his guitar and began to write and sing songs that could only come from a crushed and broken heart. Songs have poured out, and God has used them mightily to reach myriads of people. He has been faithful to share Melissa' life with millions, and is always seeking one more person who will be changed because of Melissa's life, her suffering, her death, her complete surrender to God's perfect will.

For Jesus, for Melissa, and for Jeremy, it has always been about that one life. Jesus gave up His life for each of us personally. He loves you and died for you so you could experience a supernatural life here on Earth and spend an eternity in heaven, where there is fullness of joy and pleasures forevermore. You are so important to God that Jesus was willing to die for you. Melissa was willing to die for you if her death would bring you to her Savior. She would say, "If one life is changed because of this, it will be worth it. If even one person comes to know Jesus through my cancer, even if it means my death, it will be worth it." Melissa's prayers continue to be answered!

*Sweet Jeremy Camp—Lord, bless him please. He is such a loving servant who shines with Your love. I ask You to shower his life with knowing and loving You more and more. I pray blessing upon his music record and his band. I pray it would be Yours, and You'd glorify Yourself through it. I pray You'd be protecting his wife (whomever she may be), a cute cookie I know! I ask You'd be preparing her to come alongside Jeremy and help him in his ministry. Thank You for him, and use his life. I love that guy so much and ask nothing but love, peace, and joy to fill his life. Have Your perfect way in him and protect his life from harm. In Your precious name, Jesus Christ, I pray. Amen.*

Melissa prayed for Jeremy's wife often— "a cute cookie, I know!" When I read this in her journal, I knew that Melissa was an answer to that prayer, and that Adrienne was the completed fulfillment of Melissa's prayer for Jeremy. Jeremy met Adrienne Liesching while on his first tour, "Festival Con Dios." She was the lead singer of the band The Benjamin Gate and was also on the same tour. I remember her telling me that she had experienced the death of a very close friend and that Jeremy's loss and hers was something that God used to bond them together. On the outside she was very different from Melissa, a punk rocker with purple hair and a South African accent. On the inside she was very similar, a huge compassionate heart, a crazy, consuming, growing love for Jesus and for Jeremy. Perfect! A very "cute cookie" and an answer to Melissa's prayers and mine.

The Lord gave me an incredible dream just shortly before Jeremy and Adrienne's wedding. Melissa and I were running towards a church. She kept saying, "Hurry up, Mom, we're late!" We rushed into the back foyer of the church just in time to see Adrienne before she walked down the aisle. Her dress was beautiful, she was beautiful, and Melissa was so happy and excited. We slipped into the back of the church and stood in the rear. Melissa said, "She is so beautiful, Mom." We watched the entire ceremony, and after Jeremy kissed his bride they started to dance. There was great joy in all the people, and Melissa and I jumped and danced for joy.

*"You have turned for me my mourning into dancing; You have put off my sackcloth and clothed me with gladness, To the end that my glory may sing praise to You and not be silent. O Lord my God, I will give thanks to You forever."*

—Psalm 30:11-12

*"When I cross over Jordan, I'm gonna sing, gonna shout
I'm gonna look into Your eyes and see, You never let me down
So take me on the pathway that will lead me home to You."*

"If you Want Me To" Written by Ginny Owens and
Kyle David Matthews

# CHAPTER

15

## THE SUPERNATURAL

*"Lord, will you tell Melissa I love her? Will you shout it across the heavens, 'Melissa, Mom loves you!' I don't know if that is possible, Lord, but I just want to tell her over and over again, I love you!"*

My day began overwhelmed with sorrow. I found myself, again, alone in the house. I pulled out our photograph bins. We have lots of them. My daughters loved to take pictures, but organizing them was not a part of their joy nor mine. The pictures from infancy to adulthood found themselves in large plastics bins and photo boxes. I started looking through the photos with the thought that I would organize all of Melissa's. With each photo, I was being thrown into deeper and deeper mourning. My broken heart continued to cry out to the Lord, "Jesus, please tell Lis I love her."

This child of mine was so much a part of me that I couldn't separate us. My children are all precious to me and have a deep grip on my heart, but Melissa's grip was like a vise that couldn't be loosed. What differed wasn't that my love was greater for her, it was her great love for me. I know she knew I loved her, but did I say it enough? Did she hear it enough? I continued throughout the day, asking Jesus to tell her that I loved her. A strange thought came into my head. Well, not really a thought, but that familiar voice, saying, "Janette, look in your top desk drawer."

*What? No, I'm sitting on the floor weeping, and I'm staying here in my sorrow— there is nothing in my desk that I need to see. My desk is a mess, and my top drawer is like a junk drawer.* That is what I was thinking. I went back to weeping. "Shout it across the heavens, Lord, 'Melissa, Mom loves you!'"

"Go look in your desk!" I continued to shake off that voice until it was a continual dripping that I couldn't ignore. I finally got up and went to my desk. I opened the top drawer, and there sat a note. It was the last note that Melissa had written me before she died. On the outside of the note, Melissa had written, "Mommy, I love you!" I knew Jesus was telling me that He did tell Melissa that I loved her, He did shout it across the heavens, and she was answering, "Jesus, please tell Mom that I love her!" I am overcome with the sweetness of my Lord and Savior. He truly is close to the brokenhearted. He truly comforts those who mourn.

As I pondered that encounter, I was reminded of the Scriptures that say we are hidden with Christ in God, and that God has raised us up together and made us sit together in heavenly places in Christ Jesus (Colossians 3:3; Ephesians 2:6). Wow! We are hidden with Christ in God. We have been raised up together, and we are sitting together in the heavenly places in Christ Jesus. Heaven—what and amazing thought to take the place of my reality! It's just behind the veil, in a dimension that is hidden from us. It's not far away, but very, very close to us. Thoughts began to flood my mind. Jesus prayed that we would be one as He and the Father are one. The truth is, I am one with Melissa. I am hidden in Christ with her. I am sitting together with her in the heavenly places in Christ Jesus. I can't see it, but it is my position, and she is there, too. The Lord used these Scriptures to assure me that Melissa's grip on me did not need to be loosed. I didn't need to separate from her. The bond we had still existed! The love we shared was as strong as ever, if not stronger! We are still very connected, and it will be that way throughout eternity.

The Lord continued to give me reminders of my eternal connection with Melissa, especially when I was caught up in sorrow. The first year, wading through grief was daunting and full of challenges, but also full of God encounters as He made Himself very real to me. My husband, Mark, had taken an associate pastor position at The Rock Church, where we had been attending with Melissa. On Sundays he was gone from early in the morning to late at night. I often found myself attending church alone. I liked to go to the 7 p.m. service because it was the service Melissa went to, and it was full of young people. One night I parked my car and began walking to the campus of Cal State San Diego where the church met. It was dark and foggy. As I was watching the fog, I was musing on the veil that separates us from seeing heaven and so wishing I could get just a little glimpse. I found a seat just as worship began. I often have tears roll down my cheeks during worship as I feel the touch of the Holy Spirit on me. But this night was more intense—I was overcome with grief and began to weep. I had that heaving thing going on; it was that kind of weeping.

> **MOM!** *Sing with me!*
> *I'm singing at the feet of Jesus!*

It was Melissa's voice, as if she was standing right next to me. Loud and strong, "Sing with me, Mom!" I could hear Melissa singing, and I began to sing with all my heart right along with her. I could hear a choir in heaven joining her. It was amazing, and transported me out of grief into the glories of heaven.

As we sat down, the woman seated next to me took hold of my arm and said, "That was amazing. You have such a beautiful voice!" I smiled and thought, "You weren't hearing me, you were hearing Melissa and the voices of heaven!" I love to sing, but I don't have that great of a voice. For a moment the Lord lifted the veil and allowed me to hear Melissa and the voices of heaven singing at His feet.

I am now a fervent worshiper. Whether in church, my car, or at home, I will sing praises and lift my hands in adoration and worship for all that my Savior has done to give me eternal life. Worship heals every sorrow every time.

*I want to praise You, Jesus. You are so amazing to me. You are honey to my lips and water to my soul. You are the love of my life.*

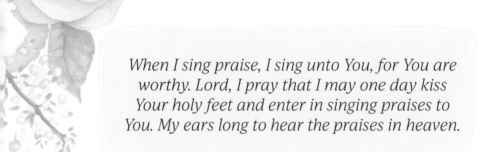

*When I sing praise, I sing unto You, for You are worthy. Lord, I pray that I may one day kiss Your holy feet and enter in singing praises to You. My ears long to hear the praises in heaven.*

*Who could complain? No one will criticize the worship team in heaven. I pray that You'll fill us down on Earth with the knowledge of Your praises.*

I was caught up in awe and wonder—in awe of the wonder of heaven, the place that Jesus prepared for Melissa and is still preparing for me. In awe of God, who supernaturally revealed Himself to me. In awe of His Word, the Bible that always brings comfort to me. In awe of the showers of love He lavishly poured out on me. And in awe and amazement of my daughter as I learned more about her through her journals.

I knew Melissa well. I had observed her life and her walk with God. I had seen the glory of God glowing from her face when she was miraculously healed and the same glow radiating through her in the midst of great suffering. She experienced the heights of joy in falling in love with and marrying the man she had longed for and prayed for. She also experienced the depths of pain, suffering, and disappointment. Her spiritual and psychological well-being did not fluctuate with her circumstances. Whether it was in the best of times or the worst of times, she was always thinking of other people and ready to share with them all that God was doing in her life. People mattered to her. She loved them—really loved them—doctors, nurses, hospital staff, her friends, family, and Jeremy.

I thought I knew Melissa well, but she continued to astound me in her life and even more through her journals. The Lord opened my eyes to the extraordinary, the supernatural, the mysterious, the unexplainable. God intends for us to have a life like that—a supernatural, abundant life where He is alive and working in every detail, teaching us how to live and bringing us into His glory.

I thought about the great love I saw in her life and the supernatural joy that filled her, and I remembered that even as a little girl Melissa was drawn to Jesus. At the age of five she heard the song "El Shaddai" by Amy Grant. It was the greatest song she ever heard, and it brought her so much joy. She sang it all the time, and that was how she became a worshiper of God. God was preparing her even then for her husband Jeremy and the amazing life that was ahead of her as His worshiper.

When Melissa was in high school, her relationship with Jesus intensified. She had accepted Jesus as her Savior when she was a child, and now at fifteen, she desired to know Him at a deeper level. Her Bible and her journals became her constant companions.

Melissa lived out the call of Christ:

*"Then Jesus said to His disciples, 'If anyone desires to come after Me, let him deny himself, and take up his cross, and follow Me.'"*

—MATTHEW 16:24

She committed her life to being a follower of Jesus. Wherever He led, whatever He asked, she was all in. No turning back!

*I can trust my needs to be met by my heavenly Father. I am now free to love and serve. I need not to rely on a man or woman, friend or foe, to give me these riches because Jesus Christ says, "Melissa, I have all this for you and more. I hold the key to your heart. I am the area of love and quietness, gentleness and peace you long to open up. Let Me love you, and in return your love will be evident to all who see you. I love you, Melissa. Hear My cry. Listen to My words. Trust in Me, your Lord and Savior. Let Me make the promises, and you can take hold of them. Love!"*

*Lord, I thank You! I praise You; I lift up all of my love to You now!*

*I ask that You would look into my heart, see the love I have for You, and all of what is left, burn it. I pray for only the love You have and only the desire You have.*

*This is my prayer, that Your love may abound more and more in knowledge and depth of insight, that You may be able to decide what is best and may be pure and blameless until the day of Christ, to the glory and honor of God.*

Melissa's greatest desire was for God to use her life to bring others to belief and faith in Jesus Christ as their Savior. Why is that? Melissa knew she was a sinner saved by grace. She felt the weight of her sin and knew its consequences in this life and the life to come. She was sensitive to a pinprick when it came to sin, feeling the pain that it caused her Savior. She was gloriously saved by Jesus' death on the cross and His resurrection that gave her new life, an abundant life here on Earth. She wanted everyone to know this great love that she had. She was willing to go through pain, suffering, and even death so that others would come to know the Savior she loved so much.

*O Lord, I don't ever want to say that something is unfair to me. Because on the cross (which Your Father sent you to), You were treated as if You had committed every sin ever committed by those who believe in You. You bore all of our sins so that we could bear Your righteousness. God treated You with my rightful punishment. And God treats all of us who believe as if we have done only the righteous deeds of the sinless Son of God.*

*Lord, Your love is the most amazing and precious treasure in the entire world and in all that is. You are the God of my heart and my soul. O precious lover of my soul, Savior King, thank You, and I'm so sorry. I'm sorry first of all for the sins I've committed and continue to commit and all the sins to come. O, I'm so sorry about that. I'm literally eternally indebted to You for paying the price for them. Lord, I'm sorry for speaking Your gospel as if I were painting with water. May I never make light of all You did on the* cross on Calvary. Christ, You became my bridge from eternal damnation and weeping and gnashing of teeth in hell to eternity in Your presence in heaven. O Lord, how close I came to hell, I deserved it and deserve it still, yet You paved another road.

> Lord, my love for You is the joy of my life and the reason worth living. I want to live so that my faith may increase. I want Earth for me to be building faith every day until finally in heaven I'll be with You and my faith will be complete.

*I figure my life is more than worth living and living well, for I know that I'm truly nothing without You. Lord Jesus, I love You and want You to be my Savior and King every moment.*

Melissa **discovered the mystery** to living a life filled with love and joy no matter what the circumstances were at a very young age. Her journals reveal the secret: she loved because He first loved her. Jesus pursued her with His love, and she responded by loving Him with all her heart, mind, and soul. She is still touching people with her sacrificial love today. I hope you got to know Melissa a little through her journals and her story, and that her life will inspire and encourage you to respond to the One who is pursing you.

> " If one life comes to know Jesus Christ as their Savior through what I go through, it will all be worth it. "
> ♥ *Melissa*

# EPILOGUE

*"And God shall wipe away all tears from their eyes; there shall be no more death, nor sorrow, nor crying. There shall be no more pain, for the former things have passed away."*

—*Revelation 21:4*

*There will be a day!*

*H*ow amazing is that? It will all be worth it when we are all together; the myriads of people who are now in heaven because One Life was willing to sacrifice all. That One Life is Jesus Christ. But each of us has a choice while on this earth; are we willing to be that one life that makes a difference in our generation?

When I was twenty-one, I was faced with that question just as Melissa was faced with the decision whether to follow Jesus wholeheartedly and live for others or live life for herself. I choose Jesus; there was no other choice for me. He had touched my heart. He had given His all for me, and He was worthy of me giving my all to Him.

*"I have been crucified with Christ; it is no longer I who live, but Christ lives in me; and the life which I now live in the flesh I live by faith in the Son of God, who loved me and gave Himself for me."*

—*Galatians 2:20*

One night I surrendered my life to His will above my own. From that moment on, my life was no longer mine. God has created each one of us with a purpose and an opportunity to impact the times we live in. As Melissa said,

*"Big or small, I'm willing for it all. This journey is ours—let's go!"*

♡ Melissa

It's been a wild ride, full of ups and downs, joys and many sorrows, but nonetheless well worth the risk. If my life only impacted one other life, then it has all been worth it. What if my whole purpose was to impact one life, and that one life was Melissa? Oh, so worth it!!

I think most of us won't see the impact of our lives until we are in heaven. We have no idea how one act of love or kindness can change someone's life. Since Melissa's death, I have sat with many mothers who have experienced the death of their child. The one thing they all long for is to know that their child's life had meaning. We absolutely can't know the full impact of a life, but we can know that God had an eternal purpose and plan and it was good, very good. He created life to give Him glory, and we will see it in heaven.

I am privileged and beyond grateful that I have been able to see some of the impact Melissa's life has had on others. Jeremy's tenacity in writing new songs and his commitment to continue sharing Melissa's life and his testimony has brought about a mighty harvest that I could never have imagined. I am blown away at the amazing things God has done through these two lives that surrendered to God's way and followed hard after Jesus. With the movie *I Still Believe*, based on their love story, the impact will increase exponentially. I've been told they expect one hundred million people to see the movie.

When I think about Melissa and Jeremy, their humble beginning and sweet innocence, I am reminded that the Lord is looking for men and women who have a heart for Him. There is no other qualification.

> *"For the eyes of the* Lord *run to and fro throughout the whole earth, to show Himself strong on behalf of those whose heart is loyal to Him."*
>
> —2 Chronicles 16:9

Look at what God has done and is continuing to do!

The Bible tells us,

> *"Eye has not seen, nor ear heard, nor have entered into the heart of man the things which God has prepared for those who love Him."*
>
> —1 Corinthians 2:9

Our sufferings and afflictions are just momentary; they don't compare to what the Lord has prepared for us.

> *"Our light affliction, which is but for a moment, is working for us a far more exceeding and eternal weight of glory"*
>
> —2 CORINTHIANS 4:17

In comparison to the everlasting glories of heaven, our troubles, pain, and sorrows are only light temporary afflictions. I in no way want to discount the intense pain many suffer in this life, but be encouraged that one day you will say, "It was all worth it!" Hang on, sweet soul, relief is coming, and your reward will be great.

There is a phrase in 2 Corinthians 6:10,

> *"sorrowful, yet always rejoicing,"*

that perfectly describes me. I am sorrowful to the depths of my soul, yet I have a heart full of joy and continued rejoicing. Sorrow and joy can fill the same place in our hearts. Jesus is described as a Man of Sorrows, yet He tells me,

> *"These things I have spoken to you, that My joy may remain in you, and that your joy may be full"*
>
> —JOHN 15:11

Oh, it is so true!

The Lord has been so good to me. He has blessed me with His great love for me and filled me with His love for others. He has given me supernatural comfort and joy that is unexplainable. And He has blessed me with a double portion of Melissa's spirit. My first two granddaughters, Gracie and Maci, remind me of Melissa in so many ways, especially their sweet spirit and the great love we have for one another. Maci has her hair—long, think, brown, and beautiful! Every time I brush it, I see Melissa. Gracie and Maci are two months apart and are best friends. They both have a deep grip on my heart, like Melissa's grip, a vise that can't be loosed. I call them my double portion.

The Lord didn't stop there; He added Kenzie, Harper, Tanner, Daphne, Kirra, and Kili—a total of seven granddaughters and one grandson, and all have a portion of Melissa's beautiful spirit in them. How good is my God? He gave me the abundant blessings of seven granddaughters that fill my heart with tons of girl love and one grandson who has a heart for worship and loves to sing out loud and clear about the power of Jesus' name. I believe all of them have a special touch from above. They are my exceedingly great joy.

I know I will see my daughter again. I know there will be a glorious reunion. Until that day comes, I will continue to share the love of Jesus and talk about the powerful work He wants to do through one life that is fully surrendered to Him.

"His love and His plan are so good, and all we are called to do is trust it. No matter what we think, we need to remember our home is in heaven with Jesus our God, so whatever happens as we pass through Earth, make sure it glorifies God so you can have the joy of His love even before your eyes see His face."

224

# MELISSA

# BETTER TOGETHER

# ELEBRATING

# LOVE

FAMILY & FRIENDS

# MELISSA & JEREMY

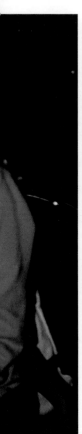

# MEMORIES

# ALWAYS REMEMBERED

So finally the part
where I told him my love
revelation. We sat down
on the bed and got all
cozy, and then I realized
how nervous I was. So
by your wisdom we prayed
and then my fear was gone.
This was the biggest thing
I ever was going to say.
So, I began by telling
him how I've been praying
for him for a long time and
his family & everything. His
face was so cute, I could
tell he was thinking "Spit
it out Melissa!" So I told
him and then, You Lord,
had put it on my heart
to pray and fast for him &
I, and I did. I told him
how I was praying and
asking the Lord if I loved

him. Yes thats what I was praying. And I told him "I do. I love you Jeremy! I know, I know." Then I was mumbling something and I think thats when he came in and kissed me. How I love & long to kiss him. I just know when the timing is right we will make such an on fire couple, that loves you Lord first and always & then one another! I know he loves me but he's just scared. Infact he said he was and we cried. And I told him how before I knew I had cancer (thinking there was like a 1% chance) I had asked you to heal me for him. & I know you have and that this chemotherapy will kill all the microscopic cancer cells left. I will not be

* Be not afraid, only believe
Mk. 5:36          Amen

*Oh, magnify the Lord with me, and let us exalt His name together*

- PSALM 34:3

**Mark, Ryan, Janette, Megan, Heather and Jeremy**
**Easter April 15, 2001**

## We would love to hear from you.

If you would like more information on how to know you will go to heaven or how to live life with authentic joy in the midst of devastating news, grief, heartbreak, disappointment and loss please contact us.

If Melissa's life has touched yours we would love to hear your story. You can contact us on our website.

# www.IfOneLife.com